Women WHO BREAK *Rules*

A New Guidebook for Business Success

WOMEN'S POWER NETWORKING LEADERS

Published by ReEnchant Planet Earth Publishing
Raleigh, North Carolina

ISBN-13: 978-1-7324583-7-6

TABLE OF CONTENTS

PREFACE

Women's Power Networking, WPN as many of us call it, is a network of women in business under the direction of Marilyn Shannon. We come together to share, teach, and glean inspiration from each other's experiences and insights. We arrive in all different shapes, sizes, and colors, yet we hold one major thing in common: we are women who happen to be in business. We know we are strong, dedicated, hard-working, fearful, nervous, challenged, and brave. We recently took a leap and jumped into the unknown—an unknown for many and a fa-miliar tradition for others.

WPN has 20 plus chapters across the country and world. Each chapter meets on a consistent basis, supporting each woman in the group. We provide encouragement, coaching, referral assistance, brand-ing, leadership, and more. We stand as individual businesswomen, but we soar as a unit of women helping each other along our journeys. We are super proud of what WPN has done and is doing, yet there are still mountains to climb and rivers to cross. Here is how we took this up a notch.

Women Who Break Rules—A New Guidebook for Business Success was birthed from our Founder Marilyn Shannon. Putting our efforts on paper to author a book, we explored and delved deeply into our minds, bodies, and souls, and we unveiled the thing, the itch, and the call that propelled us to break rules in our businesses. Eight women from vari-ous WPN chapters joined together over this last year to piece their stories together in honor of the rules that no longer live in their way and the excitement of their developments. Constructing a book about *breaking the rules* had us bursting out from our individual chapters to tell hidden truths. It is not business as usual for the WPN business leaders in this book. Rather than sharing the traditions of old, in this book we reveal wisdom and experience that is new, fresh, innovative, sharp, witty, worthy, and female.

We had a great time collaborating and creating our new relationships. We admired each other's wit and evolution. This journey began the last quarter of 2019. Our intentions to have the book completed by mid-summer were ruled out in March of 2020 with the arrival of COVID-19. Of course, this global health crisis would indeed trickle down and affect the wrap-up of our book. The timeline became insignificant because at center stage was now the impact on the state and development of our businesses, lives, and spirits. For some mom business owners, a new title of teacher was added to the already long list of duties. The rules began to change again and break in different directions.

Our new rule of thumb was to extend support to one another with patience, kindness, empathy, and love as this crisis unfolded across the world.

Our hope is that, as you read our stories, you recognize a piece of yourself. We hope you find hope, help, guidance, mentorship, strength, and influence to join the rule breaking movement by becoming *Women Who Break Rules.*

Acknowledgments –
Who We Thank for Helping Us
Break Those Rules

Cynthia

Thank you to Marilyn Shannon for her persistence and encouragement, Chris Rinehart for keeping us organized, my fellow rulebreakers for inspiring me through their stories, and my family for being my first readers and for revealing and breaking rules with me every day.

Rachel

Contributing to this book has helped me take a deeper look into myself. I would like to start by thanking my coach, Jeanie Scott, who helped me realize that sharing a story can be more powerful than the fear that keeps it secret. Without her words of encouragement along the way, I would not have continued writing. My brother, Jason, has been an important part of my life, and without him I may not have made it to the place I am today. Thank you for being there with me during all the crazy times. Thank you to all the other contributors in this book. Our group discussions and your feedback were integral in helping me through this process.

Kristy C.

I'd like to take this opportunity to thank my loving parents without whom I could not have endured my scholastic endeavors, miserable jobs, and essentially feeling lost while wandering through life during my 20s and 30s. In particular, I'd like to thank my amazing husband, Alex, who is comfortable letting his wife be her strong, confident self while supporting her dreams and crazy ideas in the background. I never thought I would marry because I didn't think I'd find a true partner, and then you came into my world and helped me build a life I love living. Thank you, baby.

Chris

My deepest thanks goes to JR, BR, and SR, my bedrock foundation and my everything, as well as to my "2 a.m. friends" AH, SL, and JR, who eagerly agreed to read early drafts and provide feedback. Mom and Dad, your constant support means so much. And to my fellow actors and authors who taught me so much in 2020, a year for the record books in a myriad of ways, I appreciate each one of you. I am blessed. Thank you all for making this great adventure called life eternally interesting and a whole lot of fun.

Crystal

I would like to take this time to thank God first and foremost for giving me this opportunity to put my thoughts on paper and to connect with these amazing ladies for this project. I would then like to thank my parents, James and Gladys Brown, for bringing me into this world and nurturing me as their daughter, preparing me for life. Both of my parents are my heroes and role models. Special shout-out to my siblings, Robert, Craig, Daralease (Gigi), Armenthia (Mint), the late James Derek, and to my niece Lakieshah Barfield who was raised with us like our sister. Special gratitude to the ladies of the Philadelphia WPN chapter (led by Alicia Grier Lewis). If I had not joined WPN, this opportunity would not have come my way. Our WPN chapter rocks. I love you ladies (Alicia, Gail, Michele, Ja'net, and Sandi). I could not give thanks without acknowledging my first partner in business, Ms. Keristen Bazile. I am a Woman Breaking Rules because of you. Next to my mom and my business partner, you have been my main truthteller from day one. Thank you for your friendship and leadership. Thank you to my amazing, growing, and expanding team, the wise master builders and my core leadership group (Cedria, Dale, L.A and Naimah, and Maurice and Liz). Words cannot express how valuable all of you are. I am godly grateful to lead you and grow together with you. Last but not least, I am thankful to my husband. If anyone knows my love story, you know my husband Christopher Pinkney is not last. After God, he is next in line. Honey, thank you for loving me, making me smile every day, and giving me the partnership God's Word says we can have. Being married to you frees me up to be creative, full of life, and motivated to be the best God has predestined me to be.

Marilyn

My thanks always focuses on my family, which includes my husband who shivers when I tell him what's next on my project list but at the end of the day does not have a chance of standing in my way even if he tried and he knows it. To my daughters whom I often think about when I sit in my office feeling like I would rather be doing something else, thank you. I think of them and metaphorically their powers send me inspiration because of who they are and what they are accomplishing. My sons tickle my heart. Through their smiles and eyes of shock, I see realization and love. I am grateful to my mother, a woman who questions till I am blue in the face and who is vain and full of life at 95. Through my mother's twin sister, my loving aunt, I see strength and female respect and love for me. From the other men and women in my life, family, and friends and those who have departed this realm, I feel encouragement and silent words of cheer. For the women in history who were slaves, abused with no promise of a future, who used pain as their model, who marched and sang songs and whose stories connect us all, I am indebted to you and your women.

Marty

Thanks to my family and friends who constantly support me on my journey to "find out what I want to be when I grow up." I am especially grateful to my three daughters, Tracey, Cheryl and Lauren, and to my sister Lisa. Thanks to my mom who, even at age 92 with dementia, always expresses her gratitude no matter what life throws her way. A special shout-out to my two friends and colleagues, Suzanne Ballantyne and Pooja Chilukuri, leaders in their own right in the integrative wellness arena, for their continual inspiration and encouragement. Finally, thanks to Marilyn Shannon for giving me the courage to finally pursue my dream of writing—one chapter at a time.

Kristi W.

This project truly was a huge leap outside my comfy box of things I do best. I would like to thank my daughter for her strength and inspiration, my son for his fearlessness and determination, and my husband for his love and for being my rock. A big thanks to my parents for not standing in the way of my own drum—ever. I think it was too loud anyway. To my bestie, I can't imagine this life without you. And thank you to Jay, Big D, and Bev for offering a new path, answering my relentless, unending questions about things that seemed so foreign, and taking the time to teach me another way. I will be forever grateful.

INTRODUCTION –
GETTING YOU READY

Marilyn

If there were a sign at the beginning of this book that read, "Enter at your own risk because the norms you hold near and dear will be jeopardized," would you turn to the next page? Would you challenge and question your current lifestyle, path, belief system, job, and career? Do you want to? Are you a closeted dreamer? By walking through these pages with your eyes peeled and your heart listening, you are acknowledging that you are ready for the adventure you've been gently hiding in the recesses of your consciousness. Here you will find friends, colleagues, best buds, and your mortal twin. We understand. We know you. We remember slamming on the breaks, feeling the jolt, and hearing the screech when we saw our lives going in the wrong direction. The women in this book speak from past and current experiences and believe the rules they have broken and the ones looming are an ordained order from the universe. Even writing our individual chapters carved out a new image for us that sparked a sudden crack in our foundation once again leading us to the welcomed unknown. Thank you for being here and for breaking rules with us. What choice do we have?

Marty

I always thought of myself as a rule follower—until I wrote my chapter for this book. Before I started the writing process, I reexamined my life to look for rule-breaking clues. I was surprised to realize how many times I broke out of the mold. One discovery led to another, cascading like dominoes. It was an eye-opening experience. I emerged a confident, empowered woman! I hope this book inspires you to break free of the rules holding you back from becoming the confident, empowered woman you are meant to be.

Cynthia

So what? I've written this chapter and now all I can say is, "So what?" People are dying. They are dying from COVID-19, they are dying from systemic racism, they are dying from poverty, they are dying from endless wars, they are dying from corporate greed, and they are dying from lack of healthcare. People are hurting. They have lost their jobs or closed their businesses, they can't feed their families, they have lost loved ones, they are ignored or are looking over their shoulders for fear of wearing a target on their backs because of skin color or gender, and they are putting themselves and their families in harm's way to help, heal, protect, and teach, and to make minimum wage.

I strive for optimism—optimism that white supremacists and racism deniers will come to terms with their unconscious or intentional biases, and recognize that there is no genetic basis for racism. Optimism that women can voice opposition without being labeled hostile and will be viewed as more than an object. Optimism that the leaders will lead and encourage cooperation to get testing and medications and vaccines—all of which will do for the economy what denial never could. Optimism that there can be cooperation rather than divisiveness from the top down. But I fear for the future. I fear that we will have spent so much money to maintain profits for the wealthiest during this pandemic after already growing our debt beyond reason under the previous administration that even if needs and biases are recognized and goals are established, there will be no money left to make reparations or to provide healthcare for all or to improve our education system to the point where no one mistakes authoritarian rule for democratic process, or that subsidizing green technology will be impossible to combat the long ignored climate catastrophe waiting in the background.

So, here is me being optimistic. I choose to be optimistic that someday learning how to break rules, whatever their source, will be the most anyone has to deal with to meander or march their way through life.

Crystal

God made every human being with a unique imprint. No two people have the same fingerprint, toe print, or teeth. While our similarities should bring us together, our differences should be cause for celebration. Any good thing we bring to this world should be appreciated, honored, and uplifted. As law abiding citizens, we are commanded to be civil, accountable, and responsible. Laws are enacted to maintain a civilized nation. There are written and unwritten laws. There are also biases, prejudices, injustices, bigotry, and a long list of evil and ungodly things that plague our country and the world. What contribution to this world's fabric of goodness can I make? What can we as women business owners share that would penetrate the hearts and minds of those who read this book? Well, we can each start by saying we are here to *break some rules*. What rules, you ask. Any rule that muzzles, maims, or stifles the voice of women. Any rule that diminishes the ability of a woman to be all things to all people on her own terms. Any rules that put us in a box or seek to define us rather than letting us define ourselves. Any self-doubt, fear, or anxiety that we as women have that may cause self-sabotage of our own calling. Society loves to label us and decide for us who we should or should not be. I believe our belief systems, standards, and boundaries are necessary. However, I also enjoy liberty and want to be able to pursue and to customize my contribution to society with my individual imprint. God made me in his image and likeness and has assigned me to break some rules for His glory. Even Jesus healed on the Sabbath day, letting the people know that the Sabbath was made for the people, not the people made for the Sabbath. Breaking the rules is simply a metaphor for us to have *no limits*. We can do, be, learn, explore, give, love, help, lead, guide, direct, own, and serve in any and all capacities afforded to us. We can remove those chains from our feet and embrace the rhythm of the drumbeat or dance to the silence. So, I will dance as I meditate and pray to be limitless and free!!!

Chris

It wasn't until I pieced my story together for this book that I came to realize how much I can get in my own way when it comes to rules. Rules certainly have their place, yet as I discovered how toxic they can be—to your creativity, self-agency, and the way you move about in the world—I saw them for what they really are: Rules can be chains. Rules can limit. Rules can oppress and suppress. The saying goes, "You get more of what you focus on." If you think you can't do something, more than likely you won't because that's what you've told yourself. There are frivolous rules everywhere, especially those that we set in place for ourselves. Let's stop all of the nonsense now. Our children are watching, listening, and anxiously waiting for us to do some serious rule breaking of our own. It's time to show up. Let's get out there, and let's get busy because most of us have some self-imposed limits that we can break away from to live more vibrant, joyful lives. Look around you. Really look. And imagine the possibilities!

Kristi W.

Sometimes we believe we *are* what we are told, good, bad or indifferent, and it shapes us like rainwater running over rocks decade after decade. I was told at a young age in school that I was a tenacious child. Not even really knowing the meaning and not entirely sure it was intended to be a compliment, I took it that way. That one word took up residence, unlike the others that bounced off me like a rubber ball. I'm not sure which came first, the proclamation that someone made about me or the inherent trait, but at this point I'm glad that description got cozy and stayed. I never saw myself as a rule breaker. In fact, I thought I was pretty good at following all of the rules until in my late 40s I met an amazing woman who listened, was curious, and reflected back what she had heard. She saw something in my path that I had not seen and had only taken for granted all these years. My "word" got covered up along the way like a week's worth of laundry, and I was so happy to find it once again. This time, I'll put it on a shelf and show it to my kids so they'll know to put their "precious" there too.

Kristy C.

Whether intentional or not, women are brought up to be people pleasers and to put everyone else's needs ahead of their own. If we're lucky, eventually we recognize that we often do so to our own detriment. If we're really lucky, once we've been blessed with that realization, we have the ability to "course correct" and rewrite our path according to our own terms; other people's opinions be damned! Such is my story of personal empowerment. And you know what?! Course correcting has made me a better, more present person, someone who is actually more available to others just with more boundaries. My hope in writing my chapter is that other women will feel that they too can take a chance on themselves and their dreams even if those around them don't think it's the best idea.

Rachel

Society has so many rules. And these rules can be different for each person. Some rules are based on religion, heritage, race, gender, class, genetics, abilities, education, and health. We are brought up believing that we must live a certain way, act a certain way, and follow a certain path. Some people along the way decide they will deviate from these so-called rules and become rule breakers. I am a rule breaker. The road was not straight and the path was a little bumpy, but I made it anyway. I'm not your typical accountant. I'm not your typical woman. I didn't graduate high school and go right into college. I didn't fall in love, get married, and have children. I did, however, find myself and happiness and build a successful business. I have had to work smarter and maybe a little harder than others. I've chosen to take everything life has given me, learned some lessons along the way, and kept moving forward. Through all of the detours, I have become a much stronger person and realized that I cannot change other people, only myself. I believe I ended up exactly where I am meant to be.

OUR CHAPTERS –
THE RULES WE BREAK

Cynthia

"Nature does not hurry, yet everything is accomplished."

— Lao Tzu

A Meandering Road to Breaking Rules

Being creative is as vital to me as the air I breathe, the food I eat, and the love I feel. I knew this intuitively from early on, but I spent many years giving in to the rules, expectations, and affirmations of others rather than finding the strength to enrich my soul. I didn't understand that when creativity is a need, that beast must be fed. It does not discriminate between those with obvious natural talents and those without, those who are focused and those who are wanderers, those who are neat and those who are sloppy, those who are trained and those who are self-taught. So, the creative urge kept a hold on me, lying in wait while I followed what was deemed a more practical and responsible path.

This path directly reflected the society I grew up in with its rules and expectations for and about everyone. Over time, I realized many rules—rules about my life in general and about my creative self—were unspoken, unconsciously followed, and accepted by default. Some were driven home by my parents without their understanding or consideration of the source, the relevance, or the ramifications. Some were self-imposed based on how I had learned to view the world. To consciously break the rules, one needs to be aware that the rules exist in the first place. Since many rules are ingrained into everyday life, we forget to question why we do what we do.

After much introspection, I've determined the following to be rules that were subconsciously or overtly drilled into me in my younger years and stayed with me through too much of my life. Unpacking these was like going through the stages of grief, wishing things had been different, looking outward to place my anger, accepting that it helped form who I am today, and finding gratitude in that understanding.

THE RULES:

- Assume the answer is no.
- Figure it out for yourself.
- Do not make mistakes.
- Don't engage on a topic unless you have all the answers.
- Follow the societal norms; stay in the box.
- Authority figures know more than I do.
- Anyone older or taller is an authority figure.
- Women are less valuable than men.
- Indulging passions is a luxury; jobs are a duty.
- Vulnerability is weakness.
- Life is easier if you follow the rules.

How did I learn to break these rules? Slowly! First, I had to be aware they even existed. Then, some solutions revealed themselves to me as I experienced the impact of rules on my life. Others required a deep dive into sources and basis of these rules. Ultimately, creativity, vulnerability, and connection transformed me.

Why did I get stuck adhering to rules that didn't work for me for so long? Although at times I felt powerless or manipulated, often I was truly happy with what I was doing and chose not to look beyond that day. It was like wearing noise-cancelling headphones that blocked the signal from the Emergency Broadcast System. When I received positive reinforcement, I clung to it and worked to replicate it by doing more of the same, seeking externally for what I didn't know I had internally. I got caught up in the moments, ignoring the need for long term joy. As I began to unpack what had become my approach to life, I looked first to my childhood.

There was a separation in my family. Kids did kid things, parents did adult things, and the only time we connected was at meals. Instead of being a time of opportunity and communication, mealtime was when my dad shared his day and his wisdom about what was right or wrong in the world or with his job or with his friends or with our choices—all from a highly patriarchal perspective. Sometimes he would tell funny stories. I remember some of these stories fondly. But the humorous anecdotes were like bait to keep us listening, and they were too few and far between. In my early years, I would run into my Dad's arms as he arrived home at the end of the day. I was his little girl and he could do no wrong in my eyes. But with awareness came disappointment. No, this wasn't adolescent rebellion. This started much earlier as I witnessed my father's relationship with my older siblings. Mostly, my dad dealt in *shoulds*, right and wrong, and black and white. There was no open discussion and no respectful debate. To him, the right way was a truth; you should know it and should just do it. So, the rest of us, including my mom, kept our opinions to ourselves and learned to not talk or engage because we would be cut off or corrected or dismissed no matter what we attempted to share.

My dad could tear us down or shut us down but would not show us how to build ourselves up. It was a tough love approach that shook our self-confidence when a balance of that with parental love, empathy, and guidance was needed to build and reinforce that self-confidence. And his delivery was so clear and absolute that his perspectives appeared to be truths, not norms or opinions or rules. I was in elementary school when my dad told me that, of course, he would pay women less than men. He explained that women would leave work to have babies and men would work until they retired, so men were more valuable to the company. My exposure to other fathers revealed that they worked at the same place for a long time. My exposure to other moms was that they left work when they had kids or they found jobs that accommodated having children—like working from home or only during school hours. Despite my experience, it still felt wrong for women to earn less if they did the same work, but, because I couldn't back up this feeling with logic, I kept my mouth shut.

Sadly, I mistakenly believed that the only way to engage with my dad was to be able to do what he was doing in the same way. Conversation was combative. I had no other model to follow. I assumed the problem was mine—that I didn't know enough—and the only way to resolve that was to learn more about everything and then plan to impose what I had learned as absolute truth right back at him. Anytime I found something impactful in the newspaper or in a book or in lessons at school, I sought to learn all I could. There was no Google at the time, so this involved books and encyclopedias and articles. I would write arguments about the topics like a shadow boxer getting ready for a fight, but I was preparing for an unwinnable battle. I was grasping at straws, believing that if I just knew enough he couldn't shut me down; no one could. But I was never ready to engage. I would go from topic to topic as if preparing for a high school exam, not truly interested in the level of detail I was consuming, so the details faded although the overall impressions would stick. I knew the intuitive sense about the world that this developed was not one that could be used effectively in an anticipated argument. The original, emotionally inspiring impact of the information I had learned was lost in my search for knowledge and logic, for the lawyerly argument. For example, the anger and sadness I felt learning that the misogynistic labor laws of the early 1900s had provided for discrimination of women in the workforce in general and for women to be forced to leave work once they were pregnant could have led to a determined, proactive, not going to happen to me approach to my future. Instead, that passion and resolve were lost in my search for a logical rebuttal to my dad. Observation and experience had shaken the confidence out of me to express my opinion or knowledge, to say that I didn't agree without justifying it and without fearing the response, to engage in a conversation without an agenda.

School was my refuge and I have fond memories of some interesting teachers in both middle and high school. Many were products of the '60s and '70s movements. We actually made apple wine in eighth grade science class. Cool. I don't think that was in the standard curriculum! More to the point, I have several distinct memories—two examples that demonstrated my lack of self-awareness or any feeling of empowerment as well as the close-mindedness at home and one that helped affirm my instincts. First, my biology teacher talked about using clover instead of grass seed for his front lawn. No need to mow; it was green. He described the benefits of clover over grass for the environment. He was sharing an example of how to think outside the box and make conscious, intentional decisions rather than going with the conventional flow. I was excited to share this idea with my mom when I got home from school. I barely described the lesson when her body language became defensive as if I had accused her of doing something wrong. She said it was a stupid idea because we would have a mud pit for a lawn all winter. She shut me down, so I disengaged in the moment and was reminded of the many times I felt ignored, discounted, not good enough.

If something so innocuous could cause that reaction, what if it was something really important to me next time? Was my mom responding to me in the way she had been answered by my dad for so many years? Had she learned a bad habit from an expert? Or had she experienced that kind of rejection of spirit in her childhood? Reflecting back, I believe she lacked the confidence to engage intellectually. But at the time, I wished she would have supported engagement and empowered me to continue to think outside the box. She could have said," That's interesting. I never thought of that. What does he do during the winter when the clover dies?" Instead, once again suppression was reinforced. As a counter measure, if I wanted to share something I learned and I foresaw potential push back, I would couch it in skepticism so I would be ahead of the negativity. I set my expectations low, in a fruitless attempt to not be disappointed.

The second memory is of my eleventh grade English teacher. She was definitely an alternative thinker. She showed respect for everyone's thoughts during class and even reached out to me after class to continue a discussion on school procedures because I had written an essay questioning them. No surprise that I found ways to rebel in writing rather than face to face. At one point, we were reading *A Streetcar Named Desire*, and the teacher asked all the young women in the class, "What would you do if your husband hit you?"

Embarrassingly, my mind went blank. I did not feel empowered to address that kind of situation. When no one answered the question,

19

she said, "You would leave." Part of me thought, "Of course," but another part was looking for an excuse for the spouse's actions that could be addressed instead. I had learned to devalue myself and women in general and didn't realize it. And I greatly appreciated the clarity and power of her answer.

In my third memory, I recall a day in high school health class that was both reaffirming and refreshing. My teacher, who had started the year by jumping up on the desk and yelling, "penis" to break the ice, used the overhead projector to display a medical related advertisement written by a doctor in an article format. The teacher asked us to give our perspectives on the article. I don't remember the specific topic but, after reading it, the majority of the students were torn between believing what the article said and trusting our own common sense about whether or not this product could really do what was being described. Turns out that the author was a PhD in some non-medical field, and the company was relying on the reader's misinterpretation of the doctor's credentials to sell the product. Our teacher was offering us several lessons: don't take things at face value, ask questions, trust your instincts. This was both an affirmation and a revelation for me. I realized I had read "doctor" and assumed he was authority on the subject and as a result might have accepted the sales pitch despite my own instincts about the believability of the product. This teacher affirmed my already developed skepticism of the status quo and authority figures, and the exercise revealed that skepticism was "okay." Of course, I had to learn the difference between skepticism and cynicism as I channeled this in the future.

Meanwhile, I was receiving another type of education in Catholic church. Here, the rules seemed quite clear. After all, they were written in stone. The reasoning behind them was blurry, misconstrued, or long forgotten, but right and wrong was in the dogma. So, when I was attending church and going to Sunday school from a young child on, I was able to consider these rules and the implications for my life. I deciphered what made sense to me, what perspectives made me sad or angry, and what felt hypocritical, biased, and sometimes actually appropriate.

20

As an elementary school student, I was only aware of my neighbors being Catholic or Jewish. Protestantism was something vague and unfamiliar. I learned quickly that anything outside of Christianity or Judaism was presented in school or in the media as mythology, which was code for false. Within and outside the religious environment, I tried to believe what I was being taught because it was just easier. And little did I know it would have been easier but not true to myself to go with the religious flow throughout life. I did my duty as required by my parents to go through the full Catholic confirmation experience. But I couldn't put aside my perception of the hypocrisy, guilt, bias, and the damning nature of the church. The Crusades, the impact of missionary work on indigenous cultures, the selling of relics, soul saving as a commodity, the disconnect with science, and being tied to a text that didn't transform with discovery and knowledge were all deal breakers. Yes, those who were on the inside had community. And that was attractive. However, adding "Christian" to self-description was supposed to connote a range of positive characteristics that I found not to be the reality of the actions of those claiming that label. I wasn't judging the actions of the individuals. We are all human, warts and all. I judged the assumption by those individuals that those not using the label were less than those who were. For some reason, I was able to set aside the authority of the church in my life better than any other authority figure to that point. Even so, I wasn't always aware when I conformed to or was influenced by societal norms having their basis in religion's need for power, control, and self-preservation.

In other areas of my life, I did what I was told. With the rules I was subconsciously following, passive, avoidant behavior against authority figures was much more likely for me than outright disobedience. Who else held authority status in my eyes? It seemed like everyone did! My parents, of course. As the youngest in my family, my brother and sister were also authority figures. They were three and five years older, much more connected to each other in my early years, and would typically give each other the benefit of the doubt over me. At school, I was the youngest as I was born in December, and on top of that I was one of the shortest kids, both literally and figuratively always looking up. So,

21

the other students in my class as well as my teachers appeared superior, aka authorities, in my eyes. As a child, I tried to counter my insecurity by projecting maturity and intelligence. Unfortunately, I probably came across more like my dad, as distant and arrogant, which was counterproductive.

My perception was binary: you were either the authority or the subordinate. There was no true peer relationship. And as I quickly discovered, authority figures were more likely to support other authority figures. So, from my perspective, I was on the bottom of the totem pole with no upward mobility, no power, and playing defense. My defense mechanism, which was also learned in my family, was to find flaws in others to make me feel superior. To make a big deal over trivial mistakes. Fortunately, at the same time, I was introspective enough to reflect on my own behaviors. If I behaved a certain way, perhaps others would display the same towards me. For example, "I told you so" was a common phrase in children's lives. I remember taking that out of my verbal repertoire in elementary school because I didn't like how I felt when it was used on me. It was a passive approach—setting an example but not talking openly about how I felt. But it made me feel like I was taking some kind of action. I continued to rely on that passive approach for too long.

Reading and education were valued by my parents. As early as elementary school, I received praise as I challenged myself to consume more and more difficult books and I was ridiculed if I expressed a dislike for something they deemed a classic. "You must not be mature enough to read that." As I sought approval, I kept reading. I also used reading as a tool to gain knowledge. Again, I believed that if I could read enough I could learn enough to be able to openly disagree with my dad or share my ideas with confidence, having the knowledge to back it up. I didn't understand that confidence was not just based in knowledge.

Reading became a tool I would use when I was frustrated with the status quo, seeking minds that shared my frustrations. I read about the systemic rules and assumptions that were perpetuated not only by religious institutions but by the media, by literature, by educators, by patriarchy, and by my parents. I sought out texts that shone a different light on realities I had taken for granted or hadn't thought to question. Some of the texts were saying, "Believe me, not them." Initially, I preferred to buy into the new because I was disenchanted with the old. But that approach was just as closed minded.

Over time, I sought inclusion of many ideas, not one rigid perspective. I read about many religions and belief systems of the world and about the connection and then separation of the religion from science in the Western world. This exploration led to choosing experiences that broadened my perspective including energy-based exercise, healing and spirituality, tying the universe, science, and alternative perspectives together. For example, my early disdain for rosary beads as a Catholic construct that somehow absolved sins through repetitive prayer was replaced with a respect for tools that assist in the focus needed for meditation. I discovered the value of mythology in the context of the times the stories were created and the value of ceremony in building community and connection. I learned about life before the dominance of patriarchy, the oppression of women, some of the history that was left out of our classroom history books. I incorporated parts of many religions and many philosophies and many political systems and many ways of life that I prefer to view the world through and attempt to live my life by. I am still discovering rules that I am submitting to that I was unaware of, and I am still educating myself on different perspectives and hidden histories. That I was not alone in seeking the unconventional was affirming and empowering. The downside to all this discovery is that on a local level I was doing it alone for the most part. I had a friend that I was able to share ideas with for a time but, sadly, cancer ended her life. We explored these ideas side by side. Other friends and acquaintances were not interested in these themes as life is easier if you don't look too closely. So, I kept much of it to myself as I didn't want to alienate others and experience the void on the outside as I did on the inside.

Education and reading were valued, but creativity runs in the blood of my family. As is the case with other aspects of society, there are rules and assumptions to simplify the world including an understanding about what creativity means. For many, creativity equals being artistic which equals an ability to draw; talent must be obvious, execution must be perfect, trial and error is absent; that creativity is something one has or one does not. Some would say that only the best of the best can make a living giving into this beast. Despite the untamable nature of this beast running through my family's blood, the unspoken rule present in my home was that there is a right way and a wrong way to be creative. I realize now that this approach to creativity was controlled by logic and fear.

My mom would draw on top of the linoleum table with a pencil while we played cards or games. She would sketch beautiful women's faces or fashion designs or paisley abstracts. She had attended the High School of the Industrial Arts in NYC and wanted to be a fashion designer. After one semester at the Fashion Institute of Technology (FIT), she says she couldn't afford to purchase the required pair of scissors, so she dropped out and went to work. Hmm. The advantage of the linoleum tabletop was that it could be erased so easily and no one would be able to judge what was there.

My dad started whittling at some point in his young life, became a photographer in the Air Force during the Korean War, and helped with drawing and inking comics for his cousin who was employed as an inker by a newspaper, Marvel, and DC Comics for many years. When my dad did not receive the support he wanted from his cousin to pursue this career under his own name, he became a draftsman and went into the engineering program at Grumman Aerospace. Over the years, he did many creative projects around the house including designing and building a terraced landscape and patio in our backyard, refinishing a piano, and building ornate bookshelves. He could justify his enjoyment of these creative activities because they were performed under the guise of costing less than if it was hired out, controlling the outcome, and producing better quality. I never saw him happier than when he was working on these projects. But we weren't allow to question his methods. He would not be made to explain the hows and whys. Such was deemed a lack of trust rather than seeking connection, understanding, or knowledge. In his retirement, he resumed woodcarv-

24

ing and spared no expense to take classes from the best and buy the best tools, and he competed for recognition and prizes. He had become passionate and was looking for recognition and affirmation but only from those he deemed worthy of giving an opinion. All others, he dismissed. He hadn't learned the value of perspective from all sources. More importantly, he still could never see that loving what you do on a day-to-day basis could be worth more than keeping up with the Joneses. The woodcarvings he created were of birds. For those unfamiliar with bird carving, this is a medium that is judged on its exactness and accuracy. Yes, the environments created to house the birds required an understanding of composition, were creative, and beautifully done, but in the end there was a perceived right way and a wrong way to execute that would be judged by experts in the field, and that fit his need for control and for knowing the answer from the beginning.

Apparently, both my parents were tightly wound when it came to creative expression. For me and my siblings, my parents' need for control extended to the expectations they imposed on our creative lives.

My brother was passionate about comics and would draw constantly as a child and teen. He copied characters and comic strips to train himself, and he created his own superhero. He would draw caricatures of his teachers during classes at school. At some point my dad told him to just stop because he wasn't good enough. That's my dad, judge and jury about talent and potential. He didn't consider creative endeavors to be trainable in the same way as accounting or engineering. As an adult, I reflected on the source of his absolutism about art as a career. Did he decide that if he couldn't have a creative career he would discourage everyone else from pursuing one? Did he lack the imagination to envision that a passion could lead to a viable career? Did he realize he was doing the same thing to my brother that he perceived his cousin did to him? Did he believe that his cousin did him a favor? After all, he ended up with a successful career. Did he think that if it worked for him it would work for his kids? I don't know which if any or all of these apply. On the other hand, was he a product of his times? As a first generation American, did he feel an obligation to his family to be successful? To make his parent's sacrifice as immigrants worth it? Realizing that his perspective could have been formed by any of these influences allows me to empathize with him rather than judge him for his fallibility.

Despite ulcer creating pressure, my brother did not become the lawyer my dad wanted him to be. Instead, he did a few years in the practical but still creative field of merchandising and eventually became the proud owner of a comic book shop. He broke the rule and found his way back. Now that he is retired, I hope he will start drawing his characters again.

My sister's interests were more varied. She was always a creator. Yes, she could draw and she could learn to make whatever she wanted in a beautifully executed way. But she did it quietly so as not to bring attention to herself or cause problems. This was her version of don't ask, don't tell. She had teachers suggesting she could be a writer and later professors asking her to change her major to art. But when your father exits a parent-teacher conference and creates a rule by declaring, not truly asking, "You don't want to be a writer, do you?" and meanwhile has done nothing to reinforce your self-confidence, you behave yourself and say, "Of course not." She was living by those unspoken rules. Even her more practical interest in studying marine biology wasn't mainstream enough for my dad. "Not everyone can be Jacques Cousteau, and if you can't be then don't bother." Despite her attempt to follow the practical, her creative need would not relent, so rather than pursue a science career after receiving a degree in biology, my sister went to FIT and became a commercial designer. Woops—slowly and quietly broke some rules there!!

Then, there is me. Could I break the rules confidently and head on, or would I meander my way to something that would attempt to fulfill my creative spirit like my brother and sister? Did I say earlier that I was passive? Well, for starters, I couldn't draw. I tried. My family teased me in a loving way about my visual interpretation of the human body. Arms aren't really bent at that angle! And since I understood the rule to be that drawing equals being artistic, I was not an artist and never would be. So, as a child, my brother and sister played school with me rather than engaging with me on the more creative side. We did make our own cards at the holidays and for birthdays. But I was a doer, not a perfectionist. I was sloppy—sloppy handwriting, sloppy paper cutting, sloppy end products. Often my cards had scribbles and crossed out words. Despite looking over my shoulder, I created because I needed to. I relished the school projects like building a hobbit hole after reading *The Hobbit*. The end result was not pretty, but I loved the *doing*. Again, in my house, an artist was precise and in control, not messy. Oh, I wish I had known then the potential of that sloppiness.

I did recognize the potential for support of my interests in school. As early as middle school, I found that opportunities arose from putting myself in uncomfortable situations. I would try out for things I was not qualified for like the gymnastics team, even though I had never trained, or the school musical when I couldn't sing. I would challenge for the next seat up in band even though I didn't have a private instructor and the person in front of me did. Sometimes I succeeded and sometimes I didn't. If something made me nervous, I would try to learn more so I would be less anxious. For that reason, I took a public speaking class and then found reasons to speak in public. I couldn't ask for help at home, so I sought out self-improvement through opportunities at school with a lot of trial and error. However, if the school didn't offer it, I didn't do it. I couldn't do it without imposing on my parents' time and money, and that wasn't an option. Again, I know now that some of this was driven by my need to confront my dad. Although that was an unrealistic outcome, challenging myself in these ways was helpful in gaining the self-confidence to break rules down the road.

Earlier on, my mom thought my pigeon toes could be fixed with ballet. Of course, after three years, I was no longer pigeon toed, so the classes ended. But this set my love for dance in motion for the rest of my life. I found the performance side of the arts rather than the visual. Here I could be a doer. The rules were different. Yes, precision was important. But it was a precision I could understand and emulate. Gross motor skills instead of fine motor skills were definitely a better fit. I was oblivious at the time to the rule that there was one look to a dancer and that wasn't me. I was a short, pasta filled Italian girl with, let's be kind, strong thighs. I would not be a prima ballerina. Dad was aware of that ballerina look and gave me a lecture on all the reasons why I wouldn't want to be a dancer, so why torture myself. It had taken every ounce of confidence I had to even say what I wanted to him, but that didn't matter. Just once I would have liked him to be supportive, if not financially, at least emotionally. And, if I continued to want to pursue that passion that he would be open to say, "I don't know what the options are here but let's find out." And maybe we could have discovered that I could have been a dance teacher, a dance therapist, a choreographer, a dance critic. But once again he was the authority, and I had no skills to confidently respond. I don't regret not having a career related to dance as I have continued dancing on and off throughout my life as a hobby. Rather, I regret the distance created between me and my father by his ongoing lack of emotional support and his dismissiveness of my interests.

I did the behind-the-scenes theater thing in middle and high school. I even headed in that direction in college just to stay close to the environment in which I felt most comfortable. But I couldn't see my path clearly. Eventually, classes in scenic design led to a curiosity about architecture as a career. And subconsciously I thought I would be following the rules of a more practical path and it would be so much easier. Hah! Architecture is a visual art. It's creative and precise and demanding and controlling, and my sloppiness would come back to haunt me. I tried to follow all the rules. I would listen to the professors; I would take extra classes, but in the end, despite being praised for excelling at the conceptual process of design, I couldn't execute drawings and models at the required level of quality, so my ideas were deemed worthless.

Communication is everything. Fortunately, during this time, I delved into computer-aided architectural design programming (CAAD). I anticipated that computers were going to grow in importance, and to better understand what they are capable of, I took basic programming and then began CAAD in the architectural school. I could create programs that would allow others to design visual products. I wasn't a natural at programming but I put myself out there. I had taken 20 credits of college courses in high school, so I had room to play with my electives in college and I took advantage. On my student budget just to see what I could learn, I even went to a CAAD conference with 99% professionals and only a few students. "Knowledge is power" was a rule repeating in my head. If I had continued on to get a master's in architecture, I would have been a graduate assistant to the CAAD professor. But doing well in the CAAD arena was a small part of the entrance requirements, not enough to overcome my lack of ability in other areas. Fortunately, I had gained a comfort with using computers that gave me an advantage in understanding and manipulating software in many endeavors since.

The most important tool I gained through architecture school was the design process—how to begin with an idea or a need, develop a concept, and execute. I realized back then that design thinking can be applied to any decision-making process. Nowadays, design classes are the norm in many degrees and design degrees are replacing MBAs. Did I say MBA? Yes, still searching. How could I use my design conception skills in a more practical way since even the more practical arts were just not working out? Yes, MBA. I picked the creative side of business by concentrating on marketing. But still passively challenging the status quo by appreciating that business is greater than the great US of A (a perspective that was underappreciated at that time), I added an International Trade Concentration through an MA in geography since the business school didn't offer international business. I was tapping into what I had been told I was more naturally good at, the "playing school" mode from my childhood. I was molding my degree and future out of the ordinary pieces that I had defaulted to over my life. Unfortunately, this was all very practical and logical, but now I had three degrees and no passion, and I married my college sweetheart and was about to have my first child. Wait, what? I was supposed to have my shit together before I had kids. Is that another rule? Guess I broke that one.

Despite feeling like equals before getting married, my husband and I quickly assumed traditional roles. As long as he was making more money than I was, his job became more important and, therefore, whatever he needed to do would take priority over my work or family life. I took care of the kids, managed the meals and the house and the wash. He managed the yard and the grill and the big decisions. I had never seen my mom ask for what she wanted and needed and follow it up with action, so I had no idea how to do that. Plus, somewhere I had bought into the premise that value is equated with job and salary and network and knowledge, so I worked within the rules associated with the roles, and by doing so I reinforced them. I didn't know how to be my own advocate. Looking back, I know he wanted a different dynamic, but neither of us knew how to get there from the place we had already created.

Before my dear friend passed, she shared her experiences with therapy in helping her with her life and with her death. After years of seesawing between loving and hating my life, eventually leading to depression, I sought out that therapist, who has slowly helped me find my voice, reinterpret my childhood, and assist me and my husband to reinvent our marriage. The keys were allowing myself to be vulnerable, to explore the rules I was holding onto and why, and finding an alternative construct. The work is ongoing, but the process has been invaluable. I remember when my mom had the guts once to ask my dad if she could buy a UV light that was said to help with depression. Yes, it took courage to ask for anything as she did not control the purse strings. This blue light was a treatment that she could do at home so as not to interfere with her *responsibilities* as a wife and mother. My dad didn't believe in blue lights or therapy or depression for that matter, so he said, "No." I wish she could have had the benefit of what I have experienced in the therapy process. It is the hardest work I have ever done and the most rewarding and lifechanging. Thanks to the connection from my friend, I found my way through.

Back to three degrees and newly married...I needed a job, so my first was as a copier salesperson. What a great fit! Well, not so much. When you still experience everyone else as an authority figure, it is hard to ask them for the sale. I got promoted into a manager role by default, so it lasted longer than it should have. I did love the demonstration part of the job. It was a scripted performance. I enjoyed the public speaking. I was the expert and could teach with confidence. It was a way to feel like the authority on the topic.

Eventually, I was on the hunt for a more creative work endeavor within my rule-filled box. The publishing industry was attractive with my passion for reading and interest in writing. Each time I applied for a job, I would get multiple interviews, but that intellectual maturity of my childhood overshadowed my creative passion. I didn't know how to reveal my true self to these authority figures, so I got passed over. Eventually, just before child number two, I did get hired by a subsidiary of Kodak in their marketing department. Woohoo! Photography is creative. Painfully posed pictures were an essential element of every event when I was growing up. Wait, mini rule break here. As often as possible, *my* picture taking is of scenery or of people unaware of being photographed. Winning little battles but not the war. Did I say passive earlier? Now I'm working in this subsidiary as a marketing—wait for it—analyst. Don't fret. My spreadsheets and presentations looked awesome! I excelled in formatting. I created databases and reporting methods. I could find the creative potential in any task. Stayed in that role until my husband, yes, we worked at the same company, became boss of that department, and I was moved out to an even more analytical role. Enough. Stop. Time to focus on the kids for a little while and see if I can redirect. So far the only rule I truly had broken was in my belief system. I was proud of the work that I did at this company, but at its core I had been directed to this point by the rules I was defaulting to follow.

Naturally, I would find some redirection in the local craft store. I made myself a jewelry box out of foam core and fabric with drawers and a hanger for necklaces. It was awesome. Used that thing for years. I felt so alive designing and making it. Unexpectedly, my skills had improved with my patience. So back to the craft store for my next project. Instead, I signed up for some cake decorating classes and in no time I started my own business. It was a full-fledged business, registered with the state and the town. I had a tax ID number and everything. My sister designed my logo, and I could do this work from home while the kids were in daycare and school. Sound familiar—still finding ways to follow the rules even in this creative endeavor. I made a lot of cakes. What I discovered was that the wonderful thing about cake decorating is you can fix mistakes. As a sloppy artist, that's really helpful. Here was a creative job that allowed for my style of creativity: messy!! My family wasn't delighted because I had always made fun birthday cakes for them in the past, and now they were getting ice cream shop cakes. Shoemaker's kids!!

Looking back, things were lining up for me to break free and I didn't know it. I had marketing and business education and experience. I was creative by necessity and passion; I could be successful in a creative field if the medium fit my technical abilities; my skills could improve with training; I understood the principles of design and the conceptual process. What I was still missing was a sense of myself, how to connect, and a direction.

Then, I saw a piece of artwork that I didn't understand. It was a wall hanging that looked like raku pottery but was made from wool fibers. And this wall hanging was not a tapestry or a weaving or something knitted or crocheted. It did not follow any rules that I understood. It was something called felting. The researcher in me was intrigued. The scientist in me needed to understand. The designer in me appreciated the end result and the potential.

It took me two years to find a local instructor. There was only one book on the subject in Barnes & Noble and no books in the library. I found a local knit shop with some wool roving, the basic material needed for felt making, hidden upstairs. But the most wonderful thing was an online web list called the North American Felter's Network. This social media tool it used predates Yahoo and Facebook, so it was clunky and cumbersome, but it worked. I was now connected with people from all over the United States and some from other countries and was openly invited into this community of felt makers. I asked questions, I shared what I was making, and what I was learning. They willingly revealed what I would have deemed trade secrets. My first project out of my only book was a bowl that became a mess that later became a seascape. There were methods and tools to turn "mistakes" into gems. I created visual interpretations of ideas from books and music I had been influenced by over the years. I made gifts (sorry about that!). It seemed like there were no rules, only opportunities.

And I put myself out there again. A leader in the medium hosted a one-week felting retreat with 80 students and instructors from around the world. I was drawn to this community, so I went. For only the second time in my marriage, I left the three kids home with Dad with a list of instructions and carpools and schedules and gave myself permission to create and to value myself. (The first away from my children was when I went to help my sister with her new baby.)

I was too new to the community to realize that in the classroom I was working alongside felters who were known worldwide for their contributions to the medium. These experts were taking classes from and with their peers as well as beginners. They were being vulnerable, acknowledging that although they were leaders in the field they still could learn something new in this setting. I had always logically understood this but had not seen it in action so clearly, so I hadn't accepted this for myself. Seeing is believing, and several of the rules I had been following went out the window. I had become part of a network of people that judged minimally and shared maximally. I could be myself here. I could learn and teach and share and question and get support and give support. Everyone was propped up, not torn down. I wanted more of this. So, after returning home, I initiated a more local network of felt makers in the Southeast. I didn't wait until I was an expert at felt making to start this group. I was engaging as equals with those I would have seen as the authority figures in this medium—not because I could execute as well as they could but because I wanted to connect, and so did they. I created another way to do that.

As I was developing my networking skills and felt making skills, I began to sell my creations. Yes, I started another business. Then, I joined all the local arts organizations I could. Having already met some key people in the local cultural arts community and having volunteered for a cultural arts board years before, I expanded my network by agreeing to be a juror on public and festival arts boards. Wow! I took on the role of judging whether others were following or breaking the rules. What I found was a level of flexibility that I enjoyed and appreciated. There was no right or wrong. My own interests and biases had a place in the process. I experienced that as a juror and as an artist. I won second place in the first show I ever entered. Was I technically better than some of the oil painters and watercolor artists that were in the show? No, but the juror saw something that reached her in the piece, and the quality of the execution was good enough to get the concept across. This happened again when I submitted a sculptural representation of my design process into a much larger show and won first place. Why? It was true to me. I wasn't trying to be anyone else or do it the *right* way. I was giving voice to my thoughts and perspectives and dreams through my work. Most of the time I didn't win a prize or even get into the shows I entered. But now I knew it wasn't because I did it *wrong* but rather that the piece I submitted didn't meet the temporary rules of a temporary situation, and next time it might be different, so I could keep working and learning and try again.

As I began to get some traction in sales, festivals, and shows, my work was being seen by other artists, and I was approached by a local cooperative gallery to apply. What followed were eight years of making wonderful friends, selling my creations, playing many different roles on the board, learning from other artists, sharing my business skills, testing ideas and procedures, learning what I liked and didn't like, and discovering the guidelines rather than the rules that work in a retail gallery setting. I represented the gallery in outreach settings, which was a great opportunity to network with many people in the business and arts community.

When I started with the co-op, I didn't see it as a steppingstone to anything else; rather I fully committed to it and worked towards my own and the gallery's success. At some point, I began thinking about what I enjoyed most about selling my items and what I wanted others to experience through the art they purchased. Plus, I had ideas that couldn't be executed in this cooperative gallery format. So, I was on the lookout for a space that would work for my own gallery. I learned of a space in downtown Apex, North Carolina, through a business contact. Yay networking! The space was perfect for my vision of what a gallery could be and was in a town that I really enjoy.

Now it was my turn to create rules. As part of the business plan, I explored my vision, who would be represented, what items I would offer, how things would be displayed, the pricing model and on and on. These are rules that I would choose to follow as I began the business. But these rules, as I wish all rules were, would be up for review as I gained experience in this endeavor. I did not do this alone. I did not do this in a vacuum. Along with my meandering path to this place, I took the gift of experience that I received from all the people I encountered and worked with and observed. I sought the advice and assistance of my husband, a successful business executive with years of experience. His familiarity with government hurdles, business-to-business transactions, and contracts and his willingness to work with a hammer and screwdriver were invaluable. He expresses his support for my continued success in his willingness to do even the most basic behind the scenes work along with analysis on the gallery's potential future. I have allowed myself to see him and others as both peers and authorities in relevant fields and learn from them. They may present their experience and advice as rules or as options. Either way, I choose to incorporate what is appropriate for my situation at that point in time and store the rest for consideration in the future. Now, I have the final say in what I execute, and I accept the consequences of those decisions. There is nothing passive about that.

In the creation of this gallery, I share the truth of art as I have experienced it. Allowing myself to be creative has helped transform me from a passive-avoidant, quiet, directionless, frustrated, and scared individual to one who finds connections, seeks challenges, strives to voice her truth with kindness but without apology, and is more comfortable in her own skin. Art is transformational both in the process of creating it and in the process of experiencing it. The more accessible art is, the more the opportunities to be transformed, so I considered this accessibility in every choice I made. The artists would be from North Carolina or as close as possible. I would meet all the artists at their studios, see where they work, how they work, what inspires them so I could share that with my customers. The artists would be masters in their craft in order to ensure quality for the customers. The items I would carry would be handcrafted for everyday living—wares and wearables that people could use throughout their day. In addition, I would provide opportunities for the customers to meet the artists, take classes from them, and work with the artists to create items specific to their needs. Being true to my own creative needs, I would allocate space within the venue to continue felt making.

Seeking advice, cooperative opportunities, and companionship continues. Knowing the importance of connecting with my new community, I joined the Apex Downtown Business Association before I even opened my gallery doors. I joined Women's Power Networking soon after. Most recently, I joined the board of Triangle Artworks, whose mission is "to provide the services, support, and resources necessary to cultivate and ensure a vibrant creative community in the Triangle region of North Carolina." There is an imaginary hurdle in front of me every time I look to join a new group or move in a new direction. Now, I can visualize myself stepping over that hurdle. The more I do it, the lower the hurdle gets.

Being a textile artist doesn't make me an expert on all other mediums, so I continue to learn from the artists I represent about their approaches and methods for their mediums. I am always astounded by the complexity of the processes and the ingenuity and engineering required to simplify those processes. Wanting to be able to connect with my artists, my customers, wannabe creatives, and emerging artists, I needed to know more about the history of all these mediums. I found an encyclopedic book on the history of studio craft. I could have read this on my own as I would have in my earlier years, figuring it out all by myself. Instead, I sought out artistic friends in a variety of mediums and created a makers' study group. We would meet monthly, share our perspectives and experiences chapter by chapter, bring supplementary books and images, and talk about how the history related to the work today. Once we were done with the book, we decided to keep going. So, month by month, we would try a variety of mediums and techniques. The confidence with which I can throw myself into a new medium and dare myself to learn from my mistakes is exciting and a relief. I am no longer looking over my shoulder. I am no longer afraid that my work will reveal to those around me that I am not a true artist. I am not afraid that an idea I share will reveal that I'm not a real businessperson. Now, if I choose not to take on a project or an opportunity or a commitment, I know it isn't out of fear of making mistakes but rather an awareness of what is important to me.

In addition to my husband, my biggest supporters and advisors are my children. They are grown and I really enjoyed being their mom as they grew up. I worked hard to have empathy for whatever was important to them, to be supportive without being entitling. I shared ideas with them from deep concepts to young adult romance novels in order to find common ground and express with respect when we didn't see things the same way. I didn't always execute the way I wanted to, and I didn't set a great example early on for what equality in a marriage could be. Fortunately, based on our open dialogue today, I feel really good about our relationship now and going forward. I have a peer relationship with them that I never envisioned being possible. My encouragement that they follow their passion is breaking a rule that I couldn't break for myself for a long time. Now, they openly ask questions and share their ideas about my business and I willingly soak it in.

And I still dance. I take classes with students up to forty years younger than me. I know I can learn from them, share with them, and grow with them. The worst that can happen is I fall on my butt, and I've already done that! The joy I feel in that act of dancing requires no audience, no stage, no external appreciation. I do it for me.

What allowed me to break the rules I had saddled myself with for so long? In addition to the satisfaction of the creative process and the enjoyment of the end result, being active in creative endeavors changes the connections in one's brain. Yes, it is transformational, shifting the way one can see the world and make decisions. These changes allowed me to be open to reconsidering my past and the rules that I was following, reinventing my future by connecting unrelated parts and pieces, and, after much meandering, focusing on a career that is satisfying. Allowing myself to be vulnerable provided opportunities that I would otherwise have missed. By choosing to be vulnerable I was saying, "I don't know everything; I can learn from everyone; I am willing to question everything, to reconsider rules I held as truths." I found people, ideas, skills, knowledge, and opportunity by forcing myself to be vulnerable. And through this vulnerability, I made connections with people to share, learn from, and teach.

Now, I choose following the ideas I wish to live by rather than rules.

All my experience and mistakes and education and connections, every time I broke a rule head on or passively, has led me to be where I am today, so I will keep finding and making opportunities.

We can all learn from each other.

No "What ifs?" They just keep me caught in the past and who's to say life would have been better? Better in whose eyes?

Trust my instincts. Follow them and see where they lead.

Rules are contextual and need to change with a changing environment.

Figure out what I don't know that I want to know and find people or sources to learn from.

I am an artist. I am creative.

Inevitably, I will be confronted with external rules in the future. Here is how I strive to face them. Just because the standard is known or moving in a particular direction does not mean I need to follow. Instead, I assess the rule. Just because everyone else is doing it doesn't mean it works for me, but I will consider it. Just because it is the path of least resistance does not mean it is my path. But I will check it all out because there is a nugget of wisdom in every rule even if it is just in understanding the source.

RACHEL

BE YOU, AND DON'T BE AFRAID

I have always been a private person, and sharing the intimate details of my life gives me anxiety. The decision to take part in this book was so exciting when I first heard of the opportunity. Then I began the process of writing. As I started to tell my story, I wasn't so sure if I wanted to continue and make public some things I would need to share. As the anxiety of revealing the details of my life became too much for me to handle, I wanted to stop writing and decline this opportunity.

At that point, I decided to do some soul searching. I asked myself why I initially felt excited to write this book. The answer was that my story might help someone else decide to take a leap and do something great. Why was telling my story causing me such anxiety? Was I afraid that someone might think differently about me? Was I concerned that by putting my story on paper it would become too real? Was it really fear? We all know that fear is the thing that most holds us back. If I wasn't afraid to take a leap and start a business, then why should I feel anxious about this?

Perhaps it wasn't fear. Maybe it was being vulnerable that scared me most. I have spent my life hiding my fear and standing strong despite all the angst churning inside. During my youth, I tried to fit in with others as we are taught to do.

As women, we have to work twice as hard at being fearless and dominant, especially in some industries. We try to leave our personal struggles at the door when we work even though they are weighing on our shoulders constantly. Obviously, my soul searching rendered the verdict to continue the process of writing for this book. I decided it didn't matter if it was fear, vulnerability, or anything else that gave me pause. I determined it was more important to give hope and encouragement to another than to worry about protecting my own insecurities. And so, with that in mind, I will tell my story with pride.

When I was young, I was brought up to believe you had to get married and have children in order to have a fulfilled life. A woman could have a career, but she would never be as successful as a man, or she could only be successful in certain careers. Our success was determined by someone else's opinions. So now I ask, what is success?

To some extent, each person defines success in her or his own way. Do I consider myself successful? Absolutely! Would I say it was easy? Heck no! The road to get here has been a journey though I wouldn't change it. Many times, the reason someone doesn't take a leap and start a business is because it is not easy. If it were, everyone would do it, right? Why is it that we fear being successful? Are we afraid of being better than a man? Why should it matter? Learning to be okay with success and being the best version of yourself is something that we should all teach our friends, daughters, nieces, and those we love. Overcoming the obstacles and saying, "I can" and "I will" is the key to finding your own success—whatever you define that to be.

I think I have had mental fortitude since I was a child. As a child I dreamed of the day I would leave my parents' house. I grew up in a home that most would consider abusive with an overbearing and controlling environment. My achievements in school never seemed good enough. If I made the honor roll, why didn't I have straight A's? I attended private school and was bullied and picked on for being different. I didn't wear designer clothes and shoes and wasn't allowed to wear makeup, go to sleepovers, or hang out with friends. I was prevented from learning that the world was different from what I was brought up to believe.

When I became a teenager, it was much harder to be confined within the walls of our home. I began babysitting when I turned 13 so I could earn money and see what life was like for others. I was tired of being different and was desperately looking for a way out and answers about life. During my freshman year in high school, I made a few friends who opened my eyes to the world. I learned about rap music, sex, alcohol, cigarettes, and freedom. When I turned 16 and was able to get my driver's license, it was my ticket to freedom. I got my first job and began planning my escape from life under my parents' roof. I had made several attempts at running away only to be found and forced back home.

By this time in my life, I had started taking the downward spiral that would eventually shape me into the person I am today. I wouldn't say my friends were trouble or bad people though we might have been described that way by most. I just found friends among those others considered misfits, and I wanted to fit in with them. I was naive and had low self-esteem. I knew that I just couldn't deal with my life in that house anymore and had to figure out how to leave for good. At 17, I finally made my escape. I stayed with friends or anyone who would let me crash for a night or two, basically living out of my car. I dropped out of high school, changed jobs, and disappeared so no one would be able to find me.

I had left one crazy situation and traded it for a different kind. I couldn't turn to those who might be able to help me because the fear of going back home was worse than the situation I had created for myself. However, after three months, I decided my freedom was not worth the price. I could not live like this anymore. I needed someplace to call home and the chance at something better. It was time to stop hiding and stand up for myself.

When I realized I couldn't be forced to move back home and finally hit my lowest point, it was time to get my life back on track. I made a call to my grandmother and asked for her help and if I could please come stay with her. My grandparents were glad to hear from me and welcomed me into their home. They didn't ask questions about where I had been or chastise me for the choices I had made. They taught me the true meaning of unconditional love and forgiveness.

My grandparents asked that I return to high school and graduate. I did as they requested; however, it didn't last and I didn't graduate. I know the importance of an education and would encourage anyone to do their best to finish high school. However, that was not the path I was meant to follow. There are parts of my story that may seem incomplete at this point, and that's simply because I just don't remember. I know I obtained my GED because I have the certificate to prove it. I spent some time working at a restaurant and the rest of the time partying with friends. One evening when I was out with friends, I met a young man who said and did all the right things. Within six months, I found myself in a rocky relationship that took a scary turn when he became possessive, controlling, and violent. I tried to break things off for what seemed like an eternity, which in reality was probably a month. Every time I tried to tell him we were over, he would hold me down, hit me, and beg me not to leave him. I was frightened and not sure how to end the relationship for good. With my family's support, I finally found the courage to escape. I was terrified for months after I broke it off with him. He would follow me, watch me, and call my house. I tried to go on with life as if none of this was happening, but I was scared to go anywhere alone or come home at night by myself.

For the second time in my life, I decided the option to escape and hide was the answer. So I ran to Chicago and had a wakeup call in life. I moved in with my brother, who was living there, and tried to make a fresh start. I met a wonderful guy and thought I had found real love. We had so much fun together, and I felt like this was the start of a great future. I found a decent job working in the office of a manufacturing company, and my boss taught me so much more than I realized at the time. This was the moment that my life took a turn to begin moving forward on the right path.

At this point, I knew I could do anything I wanted in life and was determined that I was going to be CEO of a company someday. My boss saw potential in me and began to show me the greatness within myself that I had suppressed. Just a few months later, the wonderful guy who shared my life decided to move out of state. *How could he just leave me?*

I began seeing another guy who was much older than I. Again, this man seemed wonderful and we had so much fun. However, at that point, my brother decided to move away and left me to fend for myself with a roommate who didn't want me there and who quickly kicked me out. Here I was, age 19, living in a city without family and with only a handful of friends. I felt abandoned and hopeless. Why was the world so cruel and desperate to make me fail? I would not be a failure and give up. The only thing I could do was pull up my big girl pants and figure it out. I found my own apartment, one I could afford on my own, and felt like I was finally on my way to greater things.

Unfortunately (or maybe fortunately), all the Mr. Wonderfuls turned out to be nothing more than a piece of my past. As I look back, I was desperate to find someone who wanted me, loved me, and who would make me happy. After living in Chicago for just over a year, I decided it was time to move back to St. Louis and stop running from my past. I learned some hard lessons while on my own, but, most importantly, it helped me realize I was capable of so much more than I ever thought.

It was time that I took control of my life. I was tired of running, tired of pretending, and tired of being me. I found a full-time job and started going to college. I wasn't really sure what I wanted to do for a career, so I started taking general education classes and had time to figure out my path. I knew I wanted to go into business and at that time was working in the accounting department at a bank, so my accounting career began. After a couple years, I thought it was taking too long to pursue my degree and decided to start working the overnight shift so I could go to school during the day. It sounded like a great idea until it became reality. I would get to work around 9 p.m., work until 7 a.m., sit in traffic for an hour, take a quick nap, attend class, go home, take a nap, and repeat. After about six months of this, the company wanted me to switch to the afternoon shift. I continued taking morning classes and finally graduated with my associate degree.

At this point, I decided to take a break from school and focus on work. I had been working 60 hours a week or more plus going to school. I was ready to slow down just a little. I changed shifts with this job several times and was trying to get noticed by upper management so I could hopefully one day get a promotion. I was learning the job of my manager, the department head, so I could stand in for him while he was on vacation and someday move up into his position when he went into another job. That career plan came to a grinding halt when he and about three layers of management above him were fired. I never knew the exact reason these managers lost their jobs, but rumor had it that there were some shady practices going in within the department. After my boss was fired, I took over department head duties for several months only to have someone else hired for the position. After this happened, I learned my first lesson in corporate bureaucratic nonsense. I soon realized that most within our department wore the stigma associated with our previous management. I would never move up in this company since I was connected to the managers who had been fired. For the sake of my career, I knew it was better to move on.

I took a chance and applied for a district manager position with a tax company. I had taken some accounting classes for my associate degree and had worked in accounting before, so I figured I would go for it. Sometimes taking chances pays off! I got the job and started working during the summer of 2005. When I was hired for the position, I didn't know a thing about taxes except that everyone had to pay them. Accounting and taxes really seemed to come naturally to me, and I enjoyed what I was doing. The franchise owners I worked for were amazing mentors. They taught me all about running a successful tax business. One thing that stuck with me was how they strived to operate while always being fair to the employees and the customers.

I am grateful to have had the opportunity to work for them. A year after starting the job, the franchise owner encouraged me to go back to school and obtain my bachelor's degree. Why had I put it off? There was no good reason. Even if I never needed that degree in the future, I was going to finish for myself. After dropping out of high school, it's like I had to prove to myself that I was better than "being a dropout" or "someone with a GED." So began the journey of going back to school to get my bachelor's degree. Once again, I was working full time and going to school part time.

That fall, the tax company franchise owners decided to sell. We had the chance to meet the new owners prior to the completion of the sale so they could share their vision and tell us about their company. It seemed as though the transition was going to be fairly transparent and easy, and this company was going to continue operations as they were.

Up until the day the sale was final, it was business as usual. But as soon as the new ownership was official, whoa! They began making changes to everything including the seasonal staff pay, office operations, and office appearance. Here I was in December, with tax season starting in a matter of weeks, trying to figure out how I was going to install new desks and rearrange the furniture. Previously I would have called the gentleman that handled the maintenance and asked him to help. However, I couldn't do that now because they had let him go.

The whole experience taught me quite the lesson about people's intentions. It would have been easy to allow myself to be jaded by the situation. I made the decision to stay on and finish working the tax season with the new owners despite the discontent I felt. I had stayed in touch with the previous owners who also said they were fooled by the new owners. In the end, I became a better person, better manager, and better business leader. When the tax season ended, the new owners and I mutually decided to part ways.

As seemed to be a common experience in my life, this opened a new chapter for greater things to come. The previous owners had introduced me to a franchise owner in Omaha, Nebraska, who was looking for a district manager for their company. I met with the owners of this company and decided to move from St. Charles, Missouri (a suburb of St. Louis) to Omaha. It was scary to leave behind friends, family, home—my life basically. But what the heck. I had done all this before! Once again, I was taking a leap. I packed my bags, and off I went to a new place. I learned so much during my time at this tax company and am grateful to have worked for and with some of the most amazing people. They gave me the opportunity in this position to think and make decisions like an owner instead of an employee.

Several years after moving to Nebraska and then finishing my degree, I wondered what I would do with my free time. I had moved to Nebraska to pursue my dreams, yet I still felt dissatisfied with my life. I was working long hours during tax season. Although I spent years trying to prove to myself that I was something better than I thought myself to be, I still hadn't found true happiness. I was doing all the things that were supposed to make me happy. I bought a house, had a good job and financial security. I dated some nice guys, met a few friends, and yet felt so alone. I worked so much and spent so much energy on my career that, when I didn't work, I didn't know what to do with myself. To fill the void, I started working a part-time job in the summer while things in the tax business are slower. Then my friend invited me to go watch roller derby. Whoa! I thought, *what is this sport where they skate around and hit people?* These were my kind of people. To learn more about it, I nervously showed up to a recruitment night by myself. As had become a common theme in my life, I jumped right in and joined the recreational league. When the time came, I went to the boot camp in hopes of joining the team. I found something to do with my time and made friends. Our boot camp group was amazing! We were all entering this sport together, learning, growing, and yet competing against each other. We supported each other and watched each other develop in the sport and in life.

Of course, it can't all be rainbows. During the first scrimmage with the team in January, I broke my ankle. Yikes! I wouldn't recommend working tax season with a broken ankle. I would like to think I hid it pretty well though I am sure I'm just kidding myself. At least it was winter and I wore pants, so unless you saw me walking with my awkward limp, you wouldn't know. I was out of my cast in four weeks and going through physical therapy so I could get back to roller derby. After a couple months, I strapped my skates back on. The butterflies in my stomach seemed more like vampire bats. It felt so right yet so nerve-racking. I slowly worked my way back to practice and stopped being afraid.

Roller derby has definitely helped shape the person I am today. I probably wouldn't have been able to take the leap into business ownership if it weren't for the empowerment the sport gave me. As I dove more into roller derby, I realized what an amazing sport it is for women and really for anyone. So many people who come to check it out feel nervous. But if you stick with the sport, soon your nerves subside and you find yourself part of this amazing group of people that support you in your journey. You learn to fall and get back up again, to take a hit and keep on going. You learn that sometimes you get frustrated and cry, and so does everyone else. You discover that there is no perfect: looks, body, athleticism. It takes all kinds. You come to realize there is always the next practice even if today's wasn't your best. You find that there is always someone better, someone you want to be like, and you can work really hard to get to where that person is. You see that hard work pays off. You learn to challenge yourself physically and to ice the bruises. I have had the pleasure of watching so many people join this sport and evolve into a stronger version of themselves.

I worked for the tax franchise for seven years but eventually burned out. Roller derby helped me realize that I had all the answers to make myself happy, and I wanted to be the best version of myself. I resigned my position as district manager and began searching for the happiness that I so desperately wanted. I took what I refer to as a "regular job," the kind where I would show up at 8 a.m. and leave at 5 p.m. I took an hour for lunch each day. And it was boring! I enjoyed the people I worked with and the job wasn't difficult. Yet, I didn't find the job satisfying. I realized I wasn't cut out for the regular job. I thrived in chaos and excitement. I need to be flying by the seat of my pants and have so much work to do that I don't know how it will all get done. My list of tasks needs to be never ending, and I need to feel accomplished when things get done.

After this epiphany, I decided there was no better time than the present to start a business of my own. During my years at the tax company, I realized that small business owners were an underserved market in the accounting industry. Many small business owners need help with their bookkeeping and taxes and for a variety reasons don't get the help. Most accountants and tax professionals don't cater to small business owners and I get it. Why serve the small guy when you can get the big fish and make more money? We all want to make money in what we do and I'm no different. However, I want to feel good about what I do and to help others. So how was I going to set myself apart from all the other "accountants" out there?

Starting a business is hard. Starting a business is scary. I jumped in with both feet and have experienced the hardships of being an entrepreneur. The first few years in business really were about figuring out how to do, what to do, how to make the job easier, more efficient, and how to find clients. When I first began, I was excited to just take on a client. I didn't think much about what type of business it was or the type of client I was serving. I connected with someone I had met while working for the tax franchise and decided a partnership would help get the business off the ground. I wanted a partner so I had someone with whom to share the load and thought we could grow faster that way. My partner and I had an agreement that he would focus on the sales side of the business, finding new clients, and I would concentrate on the operations side and day-to-day activities. Unfortunately, I had a false sense of security when it came to the partnership. I assumed that operationally he had systems in place and probably should have asked more questions and done a little more research before we went into business together. People tell you not to assume, but then we do it anyway. Lesson learned. Once I started to dive in and began taking over things in the business, I discovered that changes needed to be made. I put procedures and systems in place in order to do my job efficiently. I put in long hours, probably sometimes unnecessarily. After several years, the business was still struggling to grow. I was spending my time working part-time jobs to support myself and pay a mortgage. Starting a business from zero is hard enough. Starting a business not knowing when you'll get paid is crazy! Most people who know me understand that I can be a little crazy.

After struggling for a couple years, I decided the time was right to move back to Missouri. I planned to keep the business going in Nebraska and start a new branch in Missouri. I hired an associate to handle running things in Nebraska, sold my house, packed everything into a U-Haul, and made the 425-mile journey back to Missouri where this whole story began.

After moving, I decided to get certified in QuickBooks and to become an Enrolled Agent and a Certified Acceptance Agent. I ended my partnership and focused on discovering a new me and growing my business. What a change it made! You can't even begin to imagine how much a difference your attitude can make in your business. Since splitting from my partner, business has continued to grow each year. I realized I was capable of taking on a business venture and could tackle the obstacles that came up. I didn't need a partner. I needed a strong network of connections and professionals to introduce me to the right people. The power of positive thought, positive self-talk, and ridding yourself of negativity is awesome. It's hard not to take a look back and wonder what might have been different had I taken a different path. How can you really know? It is all just speculation and imagination because this is reality. The path ahead is forward, so that is the way I'll go. I thought I needed a partner and was afraid to jump into a business alone. I thought I needed someone to help. What I found was that I am strong enough on my own and didn't need the help of someone else.

My advice to anyone starting a business is always the same: don't be afraid. Don't be afraid to jump in, to grow, to fail. Don't be afraid to succeed. If you are brave enough to start a business, you have what it takes to be successful if you have a plan in place. I jumped in without much planning, and I basically learned as I went along, which is okay. However, it would have been much easier had I planned a little upfront. There is probably a little trial and error in starting any business. How much are you going to charge? How do you come up with that rate or price? You start with something and make adjustments along the way. Business ownership doesn't have a place for rigidity; there must be room for innovation and change. Learn to be an expert in your field whatever it might be, or offer something different, something your competitors aren't doing. Most successful businesses learn to evolve over time. Just because something has worked for a long time doesn't mean it will work forever. You have to change and adapt with industry and technology.

As I have gone along my journey in roller derby, it has helped me evolve physically and mentally. It has helped me achieve a better me. I have learned that it is okay to be who you are and just own it. I remember how scary it was to go to my first networking event. I was just starting my business and thought that I was expected to be a certain way because I am an accountant. In my own head, the image I portrayed about myself mattered. As a result, I wasn't being true to myself.

I became friends with a lady in my network group, and she discovered that I play roller derby. At one of the network meetings, she made mention of this. I was completely embarrassed, afraid that people would draw conclusions about me. Was I an angry feminist with a chip on my shoulder and something to prove? Was I a mean person with a temper? The absolute opposite happened! Everyone in the group started asking questions about roller derby and thought it was the neatest thing. They wanted to come watch me play! I no longer fear people finding out about my awesome hobby and embrace it as part of me.

When I gear up and put my skates on, I am fearless. I have a team of others around me that will have my back. We win together; we lose together. The roller derby community is an amazing one. We are all out to win the game, but, win or lose, we can grab a beer after and congratulate each other. There is enough to go around and everyone has their own strengths and weaknesses. You don't have to be good at everything. In the beginning, you struggle to keep up. You don't know what is going on half the time. You simply do your best. Roller derby has taught me to figure out what I am good at and work on those things in which I struggle. You become self-aware and look at weakness as an opportunity to improve. How many people can say, "My accountant is a derby chick"? My clients definitely can!

After several years in business, I started to find my niche. I thought about the type of people I like working with and the kind of business owner I felt I could help the most. I work with small businesses and more specifically I've gravitated towards working with contractors and real estate investors. I still will work with other industries and enjoy learning about businesses of all types, but I think it's important to find your passion and allow that to fuel your movement forward.

There will never cease to be someone or something that seems to stand in your way of success. My new passion: the cannabis industry. As more and more states begin to legalize cannabis, more companies get into the market. With more businesses comes a greater opportunity to help others and support a growing network of people. This is an extremely underserved market looking for good accountants who are knowledgeable to assist with financial matters. As I am just beginning my journey down the path of cannabis accounting, the future is un-known and exciting at the same time. I am certain that some people may be offended by this industry, and many businesses may not be willing to deal with companies in this industry or even those associated with it. Will going into this industry be a challenge? Absolutely! At first. I accept that challenge and the chance to change my life again. After all, I am a badass derby chick!

Kristy C.

She is a woman with purpose. She is a woman who owns her femininity in a male-dominated profession. She is a woman who will not be swayed from her moral compass. She is me and I own my destiny. Various names apply:

Birth name: Kristina Noelle Faricy
Titles: attorney, MPA, small business owner
Nicknames: Blue, Gina Farina, and Xtina Martinez (Born through a lifetime of fun, adventure, and love, each has situational applicability in my life, and each requires a cocktail or two to explain.)

The simple, casual name Kristy Cook, however, has carried me into my 40s; a name of alliteration illustrative of my laidback nature (not to be mistaken for a lack of drive), of my personal mission to not take daily absurdities too seriously, and of finding my challenger, my lover, my equal, my husband, Alex Cook, with whom I fell in love after being essentially single for 34 years. Alex is a man not intimidated by a driven, intelligent woman, a man who has allowed me to be my authentic self at all times, a man who has supported me in all my endeavors—even when those endeavors appeared to zig instead of zag with a probable, unsettling haste—and a man who has stepped back to allow me to find "me" and thrive in that space. This chapter highlights my journey to personal fulfillment and becoming a professional badass—an adventure began as an insecure, chubby, shy, self-conscious, bi-racial child to a secure, content, powerful, racially confident, curvy woman. My hope is that you walk away from reading this feeling impowered and motivated by the chaos in your life.

Youth is wasted on the young. Looking back on one's youth is a curious thing. I distinctly remember feeling at all lifestyle stages from high school on that the eyes with which I looked upon the world were those of a mature woman who had a firm grasp on the world she navigated. Obviously, hindsight is 20/20 and that "firm grasp" was really more of a "clutching for dear life" scenario! I realize now that, because school always came easy to me and my high levels of empathy made me mature for my age, I had more awareness of the world and of my goals than most of my friends (go class of '99!). That, however, did not mean I was actually ready to conquer the world.

What it meant was I'd succeeded enough academically that I could easily float into college without really having a plan for my life. As an aside, let's take a moment to get real here: Who really ever has a "plan for their life" at 18?! Yet, a great many of us head blindly into college, signing loan documents we'll be paying on for the next 30 years, because it's what we're *supposed* to do. Anyway, I digress...Back to floating into college.

I entered college in 1999 with the clarity and expectations most 18-year-olds have going through the same thing: "This is going to be a great time to find myself, make new friends, prepare for an awesome career (in something—who knows what—I'll figure that out later!), and celebrate life through occasional wild parties I hope I get invited to! Yay! I'm finally an adult! The world is mine!"

Fortunately, I was wise enough to attend the local university, which saved me oodles in loans, because I knew I was eventually going to want to earn an advanced degree (in who knows what!). Choosing a local university meant that many of my high school classmates attended the same college as I did, which has made it difficult to mentally create distinctions in my memory between high school and college. What I do remember from my time at the university, which is relevant to this piece, is four years of *not* finding myself, *not* making new friends (my old ones were just fine; thank you!), *not* preparing for an awesome career because I had absolutely no idea what I wanted to be "when I grew up," and feeling completely unprepared for a future I just couldn't seem to visualize. I *was* successful at celebrating life though—oh, those wild parties; those were good times!

Two years into university, I knew only that I wanted to graduate on time. So, I needed to pick a focus. With zero professional life experience, I landed on political science because my best friend was majoring in the topic. I enjoyed it enough, liked the philosophical aspect of the class discussions, could finish the program with my best friend, and could keep landing straight A's. It seemed to be a win-win for achieving my goal of "just finishing" without having to make any serious life decisions; an approach that was clearly not a win-win for long term *adult goals*.

(At this point, I should probably mention to the reader that I've never been good at making decisions for my life. I am excellent at giving life advice to friends and family, cutting to the chase and coming up with strong plans for others, and leaning on my empathy to help people dig out of bad situations in which they find themselves. But I have never been able to do the same for myself. Clearly, that is not a skill one wants to be lacking when planning for the future—and when spending a lot of money to do so!)

Let's get serious, what the hell was I going to do with a BA in political science?! I didn't want to teach political science, I did not want to become a political scientist, and I certainly didn't see earning a master's or doctorate in political science. I have looked back many times on that fork in the road of life decisions and have wished I'd had a true advisor to help me at that roadblock. While my life has turned out well, I can't help but think how things would have been different if someone would have pointed out the absurdity to me of majoring in political science. A simple come-to-Jesus meeting like this would have gone a long way:

Advisor: "Kristy, do you want to make money in your future?"

Me: "Um, duh. Show me the money!"

Advisor: "Then why the hell are you planning to graduate with a degree in political science?! How about pursuing a career in technology? It's safe to assume that field will continue to grow and expand and, while it is currently dominated by men, would be well served to have females helping lead the charge. Don't you want to write your own meal ticket?"

(Boom. Insert mic drop. Merge left on your journey instead of right. End scene.)

But, alas, that conversation did not happen. And, honestly, who knows if I would have actually "heard" the advice if it had. I'm fairly headstrong and set in my ways, which has not only served me well, but has also hindered me throughout my life in equal measure. So, onward to a BA in political science I went, and I nailed that degree, graduating with honors and a side of "Okay, so now what?!"

That "what" ended up being law school. During my last year of college, I recognized that because I did not have a clue what I wanted to do professionally, I needed to choose a route that would open as many doors as possible so I could hopefully land something once I settled on a path. Around the same time I was noodling over options, I remember stumbling across an article that highlighted successful business leaders of large companies across the United States, and I noticed that most appeared to have law degrees. I was shocked because I would have expected those folks to have business degrees of some sort. So, I started digging into career paths that could be opened up with a law degree, and, lo and behold, there were so many possible options. I learned that just because a person goes to law school does not mean they have to become an attorney. Law school graduates can go into business, lobbying, policy development, compliance, government, grant writing, and many other fields. And, just like that, my mind was made up; I was going to go to law school and *not* become a lawyer!

I took the Law School Admissions Test (*not* fun), applied all over the country, and waited with bated breath to see where I'd land. That landing spot ended up being Drake Law School in Des Moines, Iowa, of all places for a Colorado girl to end up. I was drawn to Drake because I did not want to go to a stereotypical cutthroat law school, and the Midwest delivered. Drake supported its students, and my peers supported me through what was to become the most difficult experience of my life.

In the years since law school, I've described the experience as 3 years of mental bootcamp with a side of insane parties only the truly brilliant can throw. The law school experience is the epitome of the "work hard, play hard" adage, and it really was *an experience*. You kick off the process in undergrad by taking the Law School Admissions Test (LSAT), which you cannot really *study* for. The LSAT supposedly is designed to test your logic and outside-the-box thinking and reasoning skills. The idea behind the test is that somehow your score will indicate whether or not you will succeed in law school and as a practicing attorney. I think most lawyers would agree the LSAT does no such thing and is instead actually designed to test one's ability to survive the first of many future torture devices to which lawyers are subjected during their career.

The academic fun does not stop at the LSAT. Once in law school, you're assigned to a cohort to whom you will belong for your entire first year. Ready for a boss girl, rule-breaking tangent? I cannot stress enough that regardless of what law school you attend, all first-year law students take the exact same classes, read the exact same case books, and follow the exact same ABA-approved curriculum. And, while a law student's second and third year may differ in coursework, again, the coursework and curriculum are the same across the country for the classes one chooses to take. Why, then, if you plan to become an attorney and work anywhere other than at a few of the top law firms in the country should you be concerned about attending a "top" law school? Simply put, you shouldn't. It makes *no* difference whatsoever what law school shows up on your resume if you want to be a "regular" attorney. The academic experience and teaching methodologies are the same at every law school in America, and none actually include curriculum that teaches you to be a lawyer. Talk about return on investment!

As such, when selecting a law school, what *is* important are the opportunities for developing networks where you want to live when you graduate, the career services support available for helping you land a job after law school, and the generosity of spirit among your peers, which will go a long way towards helping you stay sane during your three years of law school. Understand that for most, when entering law school, they are enrolling in an extremely expensive mental and emotional pressure cooker that will chew them up and spit them out if they don't have a good support system in place. Without a support system—whether inside or outside the law school—one will absolutely struggle to endure the experience.

And that is just what I did; I *endured* law school. I completed my studies, survived the Socratic method (picture it: you're sitting in class, minding your business, and out of nowhere your brilliant law professor calls on you and peppers you with questions and hypotheticals you can't possibly answer correctly for the next 45 minutes of your life while your classmates sit and listen, thanking God it wasn't their turn to be made an example of), powered through every four-hour exam, and graduated again with absolutely no clue what I wanted to do next though certain it wasn't practicing law. So, at age 26, onward to Oregon I moved simply because it was pretty; armed with hope that I'd eventually be able to find my way.

So many degrees and student loan debt! So little understanding of life!

There is nothing like moving to a new place where you only see sunshine two-thirds of the year, where you know no one, have no idea what you want to do with your life, are still a complete introvert, and are saddled with $65k in student loan debt. The benefit in my story is that while all those challenges existed in the "cons" column of the pro/con list of my life, I was also armed with the confidence one obtains from knowing they survived law school. Surely that meant I could survive anything else, right?!

So, survive I did. I rounded out my 20s working in corporate America for a year after which I bounced into a job at a small business where I assisted a man with growing a professional service firm. Though that firm was a huge success, I was pretty sure it was riddled with ethical issues, but I was too young and naïve to: (1) be certain of it, and (2) know how to address said issues. Hindsight again is, of course, 20/20. At the time, the only power I thought I had was to quit the job and move on to something else. So, I made plans to do so. But by my twenty-eighth birthday, I was tired of feeling like my soul was being crushed by my employers and decided to give up that career path.

I applied for and was accepted into a master's program for public administration so I could educate myself into meaningful nonprofit or public sector work. And oh, did I thrive! The coursework in my master's program was what I knew. The days of the Socratic method were gone and I was able to flourish. I loved what I was learning, and I was confident it was going to lead to something amazing. Of course, I still

58

had no idea what that was, but, for the first time, I felt closer than ever to finding my way.

I graduated at 30 with a Master's of Public Administration degree and landed a job as a contracts manager in the newly-formed legal department at a major nonprofit in Portland, Oregon. I could not have been happier. The money was crap, but the personal satisfaction was immense. And I'd landed a job that allowed me to use both my graduate degrees, despite my assumption that I was going to have to walk away from the law if I wanted to be happy.

Every day I went to work, I felt like I was making the world a better place for my community and I was truly satisfied. I loved the organization, its mission, the people I worked with, including the world's best boss, and the work I was doing. I felt like I could stay in that position for the entirety of my career and look back at my life feeling accomplished. But, alas, fate had other plans for me, including teaching me with a huge heavy hand that the only thing that's constant in life is change.

That hand of fate decided it was best to disrupt my world while I was celebrating my youth in Las Vegas. After a wonderfully fun night out with my friends, I received a telephone call from my boss' boss informing me that when I arrived back at work the following week things would be different. Apparently, my employer (and soon I) was being thrust into our own version of the movie *Catch Me If You Can*. As it turned out, my beloved boss had been lying about being an attorney, and the legal department where I worked as a contracts manager was going to be completely upended. I literally felt like my little world had been shattered. I was devastated that I hadn't picked up on my boss' lie; we worked together in a tiny space and grew very close. How could I miss his lies?! I was scared that I was going to lose my job, I was mad that someone could mislead such a wonderful organization, and I was confused as to how such a lie could not be spotted sooner by my employer (or by me!).

The next few weeks were beyond stressful; little did I know how much the course of my life would change as a result of my boss' lies. Once we were all able to deal with our emotions and sort out the mess,

I was invited to take my former boss' position as Director of Legal Affairs. Of course, that meant that I would need to take the bar exam, and, if successful, meant that I would become a lawyer, something I never saw myself doing and had actively avoided since graduating from law school. Looking back now, it is a good thing I'm stubborn. At the time, I could not fathom someone else coming in and replacing my former boss, stepping in to lead a department I'd helped create and bossing me around in the process. So, as a matter of pride, I reluctantly agreed, and the next thing I knew I'd locked myself up in my house for three months to study for the bar exam (yet another torturous exercise).

And, what do you know? I passed the bar! I could forever call myself an attorney, which was an accomplishment I didn't realize I actually wanted. Awesome! So, now what? Oh, yeah, the weight of a $35 million a year nonprofit was resting on my shoulders as a newbie lawyer—sweet! Cue the never-ending stress. From that point on, I became a fiduciary of my employer and with that came tremendous pressure. The organization was as legally complex as an organization can be, and there I was, along with one other staff attorney, tasked with keeping it safe.

I'm not going to lie. For the first time in my career and perhaps in my life, I was in a position of power and admiration and I liked it. I actually found that I thrived under the stress, though I could tell it was not a healthy approach to life. But I learned that it felt good to have to think creatively to solve problems, to develop the legal department according to my own strategies, and to be able to shape my own path in the organization. Little by little, I was finding my leadership voice and it felt good. Ultimately, over the years, that voice grew to about 60% capacity.

An odd thing happens, however, when you are the in-house attorney at an organization you "grew up in" professionally. You may not be given the deference you would otherwise be afforded if you had been hired into the position from outside the organization. As such, leadership may have a tendency to require second and possibly third opinions when they don't like the advice you've given them. While said leadership is simply doing their job per their own roles, such an exercise can be demoralizing for an attorney. One does not feel trusted, heard, or valued. Unfortunately, when you're in your early 30s, you may not have the courage to speak up and demand the respect you deserve. Such was the case in my story, and after a handful of years I went from being utterly content in my career to entirely miserable the higher up I rose.

Who the heck am I? By my mid-30s I had mentally landed on the conclusion that it just wasn't possible to feel content in one's job. I was frustrated that I'd put so much energy into my schooling only to land someplace I felt unfulfilled. If I couldn't be happy at an organization that existed to make the world a better place, where could I be happy?! I figured I'd stay put in my job because at least I was good at it and knew how to do it, and the idea of starting over was completely overwhelming.

Plus, by that time all of my best friends worked with me, and I'd started dating a guy I knew was "the one," and he also worked with me. So, as bad as the job seemed, it wasn't that bad, right?! But it was, and I knew it. I just didn't know what to do about it, so, again, I endured (languished!) for a few more years.

Everything changed in my late 30s when people I loved abruptly became sick with life-threatening illnesses. My father's kidneys were failing, and a wonderful friend who was my age developed multiple cancers. All at once, I felt like I saw the world differently; suddenly I realized how precious (and short!) life was, and I could not force myself to continue on a path that made me so unhappy. As I mentioned, I was blessed then (and now) with amazing friends who were willing to be honest with me, who were brilliant, and who were able to help me think through my options when my emotions blinded me to them.

One friend in particular had had the courage to leave the organization where I worked to start his own architectural firm and was absolutely thriving. He generously took the time to envision a future for me that felt plausible. Our conversation went something like this:

Friend: "Kristy, why couldn't you hang your shingle and run a practice?"

Me: "Oh, there is no way I could do that. Besides, I've never wanted to be a 'real' lawyer. And how would I even know if I'd succeed?"

Friend: "Well, have you ever failed at anything you've put effort into?"

Me: [blink, blink, blink] "Um..." [Insert blank stare then a lightbulb moment as I think about all the people I know who have been successful solo practitioners, folks that I was just as talented as—if not more.] "Holy shit! I *can* open my own firm!"

And just like that, everything changed for me; suddenly I felt like I could take control of my life and live on my own terms. I had no illusions that the path to building a successful law practice would be an easy one, but I was excited that the path would be one I would forge and build for myself. Wow, did it feel good to dream again and feel laser focused—for the first time in my entire career—on a goal I knew I could achieve by taking a risk to find the reward. And just like that, once I'd allowed myself to dream, the universe filled in the gaps.

As long as I live, I will forever be indebted to a stranger. In April 2017, I attended an event in Portland that celebrates fierce women business owners. I was nearing the end of my time at the top of the food chain and preparing to begin my solo practice. I was feeling anxious, concerned, and totally stressed about my decision to leave my general counsel job. I knew in my heart I had to leave if I was going to have any hope of happiness, but I was taking the risky path, and lawyers aren't generally known for being risktakers. With those thoughts heavy on my mind, I sat down at an all-too-familiar roundtable banquet hall luncheon, completely unaware how shaken I was about to become.

As the event began and awards were presented, I listened patiently, inspired by the success of the women entrepreneurs being celebrated and wondering if I'd ever get there too. I'm not going to lie: Sitting there alone surrounded by seemingly uber successful entrepreneurs, I was definitely letting the anxieties of that insecure, chubby, shy, self-conscious little girl creep in and take hold. I was cueing up the self-doubt I'd perfected for 36 years and was getting ready to make an early exit in an effort to relieve the dissonance such doubts were creating in my mind when Junea Rocha, founder of Brazi Bites, joined two other panelists to discuss their entrepreneurial journeys to success.

Junea is a Portland-based civil engineer turned Brazilian cheese bread artist, selling her delicious creations at grocery stores nationwide following a successful stint on ABC's *Shark Tank* in 2015. During the panel discussion, Junea explained that Brazi Bites were born in her home kitchen where she and her husband, another successful engineer, perfected their recipes. Despite their successful day jobs as engineers, they derived their passion from selling their Brazilian cheese bread at various farmer's markets in Oregon. As they slowly gained a following, they decided to quit their lucrative day jobs and go "all in" on Brazi Bites. The decision led them to *Shark Tank*, where nine million viewers watched the sharks fall in love with their product, thrusting Brazi Bites onto the national stage overnight.

When asked what it was that gave Junea the courage to give up her successful career in search of her passion, she said simply, "I got to a point where my fear of regret outweighed my fear of personal instability." Here was someone highly educated, of a similar age, from a minority background, blessed with love and support from her husband, and she freaking did it!

And just like that, a lightning bolt of strength struck my heart, flipped off my insecurity switch, and woke me up to the amazing opportunity in front of me. I said to myself, "Not only do I have the education and support to give my solo practice a go, I have never failed at anything I've put my dedication into before, so why the hell would I start failing now?! I've got this."

And with that, my excitement grew, and I knew I was ready to launch—and rock—my business *my* way.

RUNNING A BUSINESS MY WAY

Hello! My name is Kristy Cook; I am in my early 40s, and I am the managing attorney and founder of Mod Law Firm. Mod Law Firm empowers for-profit and nonprofit entrepreneurs to achieve peace of mind when launching and growing their purpose-driven businesses. The firm is committed to delivering highly-skilled, modern, client-centered representation to its clients at a reasonable and predictable cost. Time is devoted to understanding each client's needs so the firm can provide clients with truly customized legal solutions. Those businesses that entrust Mod Law Firm to lift them up gain a dedicated partner for the life of their business.

My firm is a bi-coastal law practice four years in the making that was founded with the goal of being different from other law firms. I built Mod Law Firm according to my vision of how a legal business *should be run* based in large part on the absurdities I observed working with outside counsel when I was in-house counsel at the Portland-based nonprofit.

First and foremost, the firm I developed is committed, above all else, to providing client-centered legal representation to its small business and nonprofit clients. Lawyers don't actually have to be unapproachable, stiff, or speak and write in impossible-to-understand legalese to be excellent attorneys. Lawyers actually are people too, and my humanity is a strength that helps me connect with my clients on a deeper level.

Second, who says that a law firm has to be paper based, technology lacking, and so freaking formal?! No practice I started could run that way if I was going to be content in my work. So, I have worked diligently to make my practice modern by leveraging the benefits of current technology. That work has allowed me to make my clients' lives easier with virtual meetings, client portals, text and email communications, and online meeting scheduling.

Through the informality of my firm my clients also feel comfortable around me and I around them. Who says lawyers can't bring their clients joy? I am driven by helping small businesses and nonprofits thrive and building meaningful, long-term partnerships with my clients. It has been my goal since launch to make Mod Law Firm known for providing empathetic, results-oriented, and accessible legal services to nonprofit and for-profit purpose-driven businesses, and I take pride in knowing that I have achieved that vision.

I love what I do at Mod Law Firm because I get to work with amazing people every day, people who truly appreciate the help I bring. My clients are strong, passionate, trailblazing entrepreneurs whose lives and companies are motivated by their convictions. As a mission-oriented person, nothing fulfills me more than providing legal solutions for purpose-driven businesses. By helping my clients overcome legal hurdles that get in the way of their business' missions, I help them spend their valuable time and energies on what's really important—the awesome work they do.

She is a woman with purpose. She is a woman who owns her femininity in a male dominated profession. She is a woman who will not be swayed away from her moral compass. She is me, a secure, content, powerful, racially confident, curvy woman, and I own my destiny.

CHRIS

Don't Stand in Your Own Sunshine: How a Community Acting Class Taught Me How to Recognize and Start Breaking My Own Rules

"You yourself are your own obstacle. Rise above yourself."

—Hafiz

Tick...tick...tick...tick. Gawd, I thought to myself, those clock hands are *just not moving!* I chuckled as the old Heinz ketchup jingle about anticipation ran through my head while I simultaneously ran my fingers through my hair, begrudgingly admitting to myself that, yes, I had anxiously watched the clock all day, ready to make the invitation a reality. It was time for my first acting class.

A few weeks before, on a particularly nasty, feisty, rainy day, I reached into the shadow of my mailbox to retrieve the usual array of mailers, advertisements for new windows, and sandwiches at Subway. In the midst of the pile was an invitation that winked and greeted me from its colorful paper featuring laughing children and adults in dramatic poses. I stopped, rain slapping my face, and looked hard at that invitation.

Now, I'd seen this invitation before and it usually went like this: I'd take one look and lapse into my automatic habit of ticking off all of the reasons to say no. The kids are too young, maybe I wouldn't be any good at it, my workload is too heavy right now, my schedule is too complicated—you get the gist. I kept holding myself back, watching jealously from the sidelines as others took my place. I told myself that it was an invitation meant for others or perhaps the future Chris but not the Chris of right now.

An inner voice quietly reminded me that the kids were older, more independent, with ideas of their own and the ability to cook an egg sandwich if needed without launching the house fire alarms. I walked into the house and looked at the kids. I didn't say a word. I saw them, long arms and legs flipped haphazardly, carelessly over the sofas. And that's when I realized that work was less hectic and my life was too. A small voice whispered, "Maybe now?"

Maybe. Maybe the cold rain slaps were Mother Nature's way of waking me up. This time I picked up the phone and called to get my name on that list. A persistent whisper said, "Yes. Now."

I was heading to my first acting class.

SCENE I

Much of my life boiled down to putting on a mask: Be a good girl. Do what's expected. Follow the rules. Always do the right thing. What I really wanted to do sometimes was break some rules and tear up other people's expectations of me, but it never quite worked out that way. And that played out in ways like going to work when I was sick, pretending to love my job when I really, secretly didn't, putting on a smile even when it wasn't truthful, and saying "yes" when I really meant "no."

I planned to do the unexpected in this class. Come hell or high water, I was going to start breaking free of my "mom-nesia," as my friend Tracy called it. I had no idea how it was going to go down and how wild things might get, but I was open to receive whatever lay ahead.

I had been a good girl for a very long time.

SCENE II

It's Sunday night. Strangers, vulnerable, we stand in a circle on the floor of the teaching theatre and introduce ourselves, a little at a time. Some of us admit feeling nervous, excited, missing theatre experiences we've had, and wanting to get back into the swing again after a break. We are all here for separate, distinct reasons as unique as each one of us.

I am here to dance with my demons, rules I set for myself that keep me in control, safe, scripted, doing what's expected…and I am ready to get into the mosh pit.

We move into an exercise to hone our observation skills while we begin getting to know one another. Our teacher explains that we are to notice something about our partner and then say it out loud to our partner. Glasses perhaps? I choose to notice my partner's hair color. We talk about whether what we said aloud was what we actually noticed first. Some of us admit to editing our responses far from what we first noticed. We also talk about how we chose the thing about our partner to announce out loud. Was it a "safe" characteristic to notice? Many of us acknowledge that it was. I feel a tug and realize that I, like a lot of women, do a lot of self-editing. It's so natural, automatic even. I didn't even recognize it until now. I'm starting to wake up and pay attention.

Over the course of the next few weeks, we all take leaps of faith to trust more and express ourselves more authentically. We listen more deeply. Laugh more and give each other grace when we goof up. And we goof up plenty; we break out of characters we're playing; we giggle; we lose focus. And guess what? It's all okay. We are part of a collective that is positive and supportive.

I risk more. I risk more often. I hate it. I love it.

We do a trust exercise, a version of the classic cross your hands over your chest and fall dramatically into your partner's hands. Only this version is 2.0. We are instructed to randomly walk around a 15' by 15' area of the theatre and call out the word "falling." When you hear that word, you are to go to that person and catch them as they fall back. Simple, right? I am sure that in that moment, my heart alone would have qualified me for a trip to the local ER at just the idea of falling into the hands of someone I only met a few weeks earlier. I used to tell myself that I'd never be able to do that kind of exercise because it was just too darn corny, but the truth of the matter is that I didn't want to do it because I felt uncomfortable trusting anyone to actually be there for me. I push those thoughts aside and try it. I yell out the word "falling" so that everyone can be aaaaabsolutely sure to hear me and show up. Then I fall back into their hands and surprise myself...by surviving it. And then I do it again a few minutes later.

I am breaking my own rules and expectations more and more often. I constantly surprise myself and I feel alive.

Scene III

Three weeks later, I stand facing my classmates in the bowels of the theatre in a room with an eerily slanted floor. It makes all of us feel off-kilter, ready for the unexpected, which I learned, is par for the course when it comes to this class, a place where I'm rarely 100% comfortable. I love it and hate it at the same time.

It's my turn to practice my monologue—to be seen, heard, and vulnerable. My monologue is taken from a play about the women who worked in the factories before, during, and between World Wars I and II, who painted luminescent dials using paint brushes that they dipped into radium-based paint and then into their mouths to make the fine points needed to create the dial points and marks. History knows them as "The Radium Girls." As a result, many became seriously ill, disfigured, and died horrific deaths at young ages from radium poisoning.

My monologue takes place when one of the women, "Grace," learns that their case against the company is going to be heard in court. It brings forth a swath of my feelings and thoughts—justice, rage, self-identity and self-agency, visibility and power and self-expression. I love this monologue all the way to my bones because really, truly, I've felt these feelings before in other contexts and in other seasons of my life. I can relate on a visceral level to her.

I take a deep, long breath and do a run-through. I think to myself, "Not half bad!"

I am under the spotlight. All eyes are on me. The teacher looks straight at me and quietly asks, "Have you ever been bullied?"

I don't expect the question. "Yes," I answer her truthfully.

I know where this is going because deep down I figured it would. The teacher thoughtfully suggests that I remember the bully, the details about that person, the feelings, the things that he said to me so that I could in turn bring those elements to the monologue to bring life to it, to the character, and to create a palpable energy. To act. I am uneasy and feel vulnerable yet immediately think of my biological father.

The teacher says, "Imagine his face right over my right shoulder."

I know what I have to do, but it's the last place I want to go. I do it anyway.

I take a long, deep breath and start again, only this time, I'm not talking to a company owner, I'm talking to my biological father.

I hesitate and make a choice. I give myself permission to unleash. It is a raw, intense experience. I finish and notice my hands are balled into clamped fists. I am shaking, my face red, hot.

The class is silent. I can't tell what they're thinking!

"Oh my God," I think to myself. "What have I done? Where did all of that come from?"

And then a classmate raised her hand and softly said, "That touched something in me."

It was raw and real and I really did it.

I used my voice, my power, and talked back to the bully, something I didn't think I would ever do or be able to do. Feel anger toward him? No, I've always allowed myself to feel other feelings toward him but certainly not white-hot anger. Not until the night of the monologue. I gave myself permission and broke another internal rule: Stand up to the bully.

I don't know if they knew it, but each person in the class stood as a witness to a silent yet remarkable shift within me.

I am slowly, bravely seeing that I have lots of internal rules about all kinds of things. However, I am simultaneously learning that that's all they are, and I refuse to stand in my own sunshine anymore.

SCENE IV

In February 2020, the first cases of COVID-19, the coronavirus, started their stealthy crawl into the fabric of our lives. As cases spread across America like flooding water, it became apparent that our country was going to have to move in the same direction as those before us to follow strict physical distancing practices, which meant no group gatherings.

My friend and fellow author, Marty Sloditski, suggested taking an idea that I had—joining a play script reading group—to the virtual platform.

Why not?

Our meetings were astounding and raucous. In a *Brady Bunch* format, we gathered to read plays of all kinds, but more importantly we checked in with one another, laughed, celebrated joys, and commiserated with one another when the national or personal news was bad.

It felt amazing to birth an environment where creative energy had free reign.

A few months ago, who would have thought that I'd start a play script reading group? Breaking rules? You bet! Figuring out what's possible? Absolutely.

Oh, and what about the bully, you might be wondering. The one who tried to show me that my thoughts, feelings, and dreams didn't matter? That I had no voice?

How completely and utterly wrong he was.

While I'm not a business owner in the traditional sense, I am breaking rules.

I refuse to stand in my own sunshine anymore. It's taken me a long time to figure that out.

And maybe one day, you'll see me standing free and brave and loud on the "big stage," a trail of the invisible rules I've let go of laying on the ground behind me. Triumphant.

CRYSTAL

BREAKING THE RULES: I AM EVERY WOMAN

I am every woman. I am striving to be who God made me to be—grateful, blessed, and reflective. When I think of my most notable traits and genetic makeup, these three things resonate the most:

Young and Ambitious - Who are you to be in business at the tender age of 24? Will anyone even take you seriously? Will you take yourself seriously, venturing into business, green and walking by faith.

Female and Competitive - In a world where women earn .79 cents for every dollar a man makes, will I break the rules becoming a female CEO? Will men be willing to follow a female leader? Will I have enough confidence to lead them?

I am the apple that didn't fall far from the tree ("Daddy's little girl"). We have all heard the saying that the apple doesn't fall far from the tree. This is what my DNA reads. It was destiny, predestined if you will, for me to do as my father did, hustle like my father did, build a business and soar like my father did.

Breaking the rules at an early age, breaking the rules as a female, and breaking the rules as I walked in my daddy's shoes, I loved each step along the way. My mother, no less valued or endearing, is my compass, my spiritual leader. She embodies a solid Christian foundation that she extended to her children and to my father. Together they were married 53 years before he passed in 2010. Had he lived they would be celebrating 63 years of a blessed marriage. My dad loved my mom dearly and showed this love daily. I am so Godly grateful. My parents were great role models. Often, we find popular public figures that we admire and we want to be like them. Many great men and women have paved the way before us: Martin Luther King Jr., Harriet Tubman, former President Jimmy Carter, Oprah Winfrey, Michael Jordan, Gandhi, Venus and Serena Williams, Mother Teresa, and Dr.

Miles Monroe to name a few. Well, I have the privilege of adding James H. and Gladys D. Brown (my parents) to this grand list.

YOUNG AND AMBITIOUS

In September 1991, I started my collegiate career at Temple University in Philadelphia, Pennsylvania. I majored in business administration with a concentration in marketing and graduated four years later with that B.A. in business and an associate degree in African American Studies. Corporate America, here I come!

During my first year in corporate America, I was excited and filled with dreams of climbing the corporate ladder, eager to gain the necessary experience in the business world. I was hired by an African-American female business owner. Rule breaking started early for me. This was an advertising agency co-owned by two women. Not only was I thrilled to start my corporate career, I was doubly enthused that I would be working for two successful women, one an African-American. Super proud and confident as a woman, I was hungry to surround myself with successful women that looked like me.

I had a good experience in my first job and learned a lot about the marketing and advertising fields. I rented my first apartment on South Street in Philadelphia, feeling independent and accomplished. Within a year my entrepreneurial path began to such an extent that I quit that first job at 24 years old. Who does that?

One of my close friends from college was introduced to a business in the world of finance. Being a finance major, she was highly intrigued by the opportunity. Reaching out to me, she offered me the chance to get involved. Trusting her and her level of integrity, I was sold at the first offer. Within two years (at age 23), she became a regional vice president on the road to owning her own financial services business. My friend, Keristen, broke the rules. A few years after, I followed in her footsteps, becoming a regional vice president with my own office as well.

Making this leap, both my best girlfriend and I broke the rules. Who at 21 and 24 years of age respectively decides to leave Corporate

America and become 100% self-employed business owners? Risk Takers, Big Thinkers, Dream Chasers, and Faith Walkers—that's who! Our faith in God played a major role in our ability to take this leap, to believe that if we could work for a corporation, we could work for ourselves. Was it easy? No. Was it worth it? Yes.

Being young, in the early years we had to work on our confidence when it came to meeting with people older than us or even more well off financially than us. We had to be students of our business, realizing that we knew what we knew and could help each family we met regardless of how we might initially have been perceived because of our age. We learned something called the "Value Gap," which is the gap between what a person knew prior to meeting us and the difference we made by bringing new information (value) they previously did not have. The bigger the gap (value brought), the greater credibility we gained. Age is just a number when you're breaking the rules.

I remember my first year in business when I was working part-time, sticking my toe in if you will. I was one of the most un-skeptical people you would ever meet. I've heard it said that umbrellas only work when they're open. I was definitely an open umbrella—bright-eyed and eager to learn and grow. I think this element is critical when embarking on a new path. There I was being trained to become a personal financial representative. I had no prior experience. Daily, I learned the steps as they were taught.

What helped me during this critical stage of going into business? What "rule breaking" qualities should one have to not only take this step but stay the course? The answers to these questions come from my sports background and coaching career. I was a school athlete from 1985 to 1991 in grades seven to 12. I ran track and played field hockey and lacrosse during seventh and eighth grades, played basketball from seventh to twelfth grades, and attended two summer basketball camps during my sophomore and junior years. Over this six-year span, I had at least 10 coaches. I believe being coached is one of the most important elements in life.

No man is an island, entire of itself; every man is a piece of the continent, a part of the main; if a clod be washed away by the sea, Europe is the less, as well as if a promontory were, as well as if a manor of thy friend's or of thine own were; any man's death diminishes me, because I am involved in mankind, and therefore never send to know for whom the bell tolls; it tolls for thee.

—John Donne (1572-1631)

I learned this John Donne poem, "No Man Is an Island," while I was in school, and it has stuck with me all these years. The poem is profoundly saying that no one is truly self-sufficient. Everyone must rely on the company of others to thrive, progress, grow, change, prosper, and succeed!

My coaches played significant roles in my ability to do that. The definition of a coach is someone skilled to cultivate, teach, inspire, uplift an athlete (student) to perform at acceptable levels in their field of study. I remember my early coaches when I was a young teen being encouraging. They poured belief in me that I could do the task. I recall practices and the drills we did early on to become good players of the game.

FEMALE AND COMPETITIVE

"Idle time is the devil's playground."

It did not matter which sport I played; I had a strong personal desire to be good at it. As a track runner, I was a short distance sprinter. I ran the 100, 200, and 400-meter dash. My best race was the 200. I came to practice with a daily mission to get better. I had a strong commitment to follow the coach, run the coach's plays, and accept whatever form of workout the coach requested. I was not the top sprinter, which, in it of itself, became a motivator for me. I got better little by little, gaining the opportunity to run in the Penn Relays (an extremely popular Philadelphia track tournament).

I was coached by my schoolteachers in field hockey and lacrosse, probably my best performing sports, so my coaches had dual roles.

76

They coached me in the classroom from 8 a.m. to 3 p.m. then coached me again on the sports field from 3 to 6 p.m. My teacher coaches had my back academically and now athletically. The correlation of how well I performed in the classroom and how well I performed on the field became very apparent to me. One of my greatest desires as a young teen was to be active in positive activities, so I stayed productive and busy, engaged in progressive programs (no idle time). I traveled in circles of people who were about something. I sought intellectual stimulation and athletic development. I believe being an athlete can teach some of the greatest lessons of life.

I moved on to basketball initially for the wrong reasons. I decided to focus on basketball solely during my high school years. Basketball was the most popular of the sports that I played. I wanted to be cool and, as a young girl, close to the boys. (Shhh, don't tell anybody.) Everyone came to the basketball games. While part of my initial reason to focus on basketball was a bit shallow, I quickly became profoundly serious about the game. I fell in love with it. As a freshman during the season, I got moved to the junior varsity squad, where typically tenth graders started. I then played varsity basketball. Typically, coaches select two team captains; however, my coach selected three. We had two dynamic ball players on our team, each averaging 20 plus points per game. Then there was me, a fast, hardworking defensive player that was 100% coachable to my coach. As a result, I was selected as a third captain of our team.

Over the summer of my sophomore and junior years, I attended two basketball camps. One was a Christian basketball camp which nurtured me spiritually (extremely important), physically, and mentally (also tremendously important). At the second camp I attended, coaches started by dividing us into two teams, red and blue, and they let us play. The purpose of this game was to determine what type of player each of us was—beginner, intermediate, or advanced. I was deemed intermediate.

I thought to myself, "Me, intermediate? Unacceptable."

It was the summer before my senior year of high school, and I was attending an incredibly competitive basketball camp. Two of the star players from my high school (my co-captains) also attended. Without question, both of those young ladies were drafted to the advanced team. I, on the other hand, was drafted to the intermediate team. Needless to say, I was not happy nor content with this outcome. Time to break the rules. Nothing I did came easily for me; I had to fight for everything I got. I immediately went into beast mode at every practice and during every drill—so much so that I went to the basketball courts to practice by myself nightly. The camp had excellent lighting at night on the court. I practiced every drill taught that day for a few hours that night. Unbeknownst to me, I am being watched by coaches, other players, etc. Before the end of camp, I was moved from the intermediate team to the advanced team and given the most improved player award. My attitude was that being placed on the intermediate team was unacceptable and to God be the glory if I should succeed. I was recognized and promoted because I chose not to settle.

From the Basketball Court to the Boardroom

Coaching was everything to me. It formed me, inspired me, stretched and molded me into the woman I am today. While I did not continue athletics in college, all I learned prior served me well during my collegiate years. Lessons learned manifested in the forms of leadership, persistence, mental toughness, faith, dedication, and loyalty. These traits continue to serve me well in business.

"Keep Your Eyes on the Prize"

After college, my eyes were wide open and firmly fixed on the prize of joining the ranks of Corporate America and rising on the corporate ladder. I initially set out to become a force to be reckoned with in the corporate world as a high-level employee. I was determined, eager, and motivated to pursue this dream. The height of the dream was to move to New York, becoming the minority marketing director of a mega corporation. I wanted to be Ms. Crystal C. Brown, minority marketing director, Coca-Cola, USA. As exciting as that sounded, a new direction emerged. While I intended to travel the world, going from boardroom to boardroom helping the world to effectively target-market to minority consumers, God shifted my drive toward entrepreneurship, breaking the rules.

My ancestors during the 1960s sang this song titled above:

Paul and Silas thought they were lost.
Dungeon shook and the chains came off.
Keep your eyes on the prize, hold on.

Freedom's name is mighty sweet
And soon we're gonna meet.
Keep your eyes on the prize, hold on.

I desired freedom. I thought I wanted a top position within a corporation, but I later found out I genuinely wanted to hold the top position in my own company. Although I thought I wanted to represent African-American people and minority markets within a big corporation, I later realized I wanted to empower African-American people and minority communities everywhere. I had thought I would influence people to purchase a product from a company, but I came to see that my purpose was to guide people to believe in themselves, to start and run their own businesses, becoming financially independent. The product I now sell is *freedom*.

The reach I now have is so much greater and more impactful. God's hand on the true calling of my life was present, and that calling has been coming to fruition by breaking the rules. Long ago I felt within my spirit a desire to be a person of impact, a game changer, the go-to person in my family. Those desires are just as strong today as they were the day God planted that in my heart. The passion that my ancestors embodied for the fight for freedom has transferred to me. I am a proud recipient of this mission and calling.

I am the apple that didn't fall far from the tree. I am Daddy's little girl.

"JB believed in being on time. He worked 20 years for the Upper Merion School District, never late one time. He believed in hard work. Once, he even went on to a job site and made himself a job. He acted like he was supposed to be there and they hired him."

—Gladys D. Brown

This quote from my mother reveals how dedicated my father was to building his business. The pinnacle of this path that I have taken is the reflection of my father that runs deep within me in this entrepreneurial space. My father became an entrepreneur many years before my sisters and I were born. I am the youngest of six children (three girls and three boys). My brothers are old enough to be my father. There are eight years between my youngest brother and my oldest sister. My mother and father married at 20 and 22 years of age respectively. By age 24, my dad started cleaning offices part-time in the evenings.

Well, look at that. My father broke the rules first. Would you believe me if I told you I did not know this amazing Brown family history fact until I literally wrote these very words for this story? By interviewing my mom about my dad's entrepreneurial history and crunching numbers to get the timelines down, it was in that moment that God revealed that my father and I started both of our businesses at the very same age. Words cannot express how much more special this special story is to me. Just when I already felt that I was the apple that didn't fall far from the tree, I found out that I fell from that tree at the exact same age.

In 1959, James Brown Janitorial Services began. Dad was a pioneer (black, white or other) as an entrepreneur. He started his cleaning business light years before it was popular. He even had his own truck with his name on it. This too was not widely common for anyone in our community to have at that time. From 1959 to 1974, he worked his business nightly, cleaning commercial offices. Dad established a great reputation and was known for being reliable, dependable, and on time. (I do pretty well with the first two traits but am still working on the third).

The quote above from my mom perfectly describes my father's work ethic. I too am known for my work ethic, and I have my father to thank for that. My dad was a hustler. He worked a steady job and ran a business. He didn't believe in just having enough to make the bills monthly (living beyond the bills). He was innovative, resourceful, and business savvy, bringing in multiple streams of income. Go ahead, Dad; do that!

By the 1970s, Dad changed the name of his business to I and D Cleaning Services, which stood for Industrial and Domestic Cleaning Services. He hired a staff including my eldest brother, my mom, other relatives, and friends. My dad negotiated his own cleaning contracts. Prospecting businesses in the area, he picked up two contracts in particular that he held for over 20 years. In addition to this, my mom, alongside him, was offered a domestic cleaning job from the owner of one of those commercial properties. She maintained that contract for 12 years. My father ran his business until he became ill with cancer in 2010. My mom and my brother ran the business for a little while after my dad passed. Overall, my father's cleaning business existed for an amazing 51 years, holding a minimum of 12 commercial and domestic contracts over that span of time. He was a red-hot trailblazer as a black man coming up during the civil rights era. One of the first and longest black businessmen in our community, my father led the way so many years later I could break the rules.

As I close and continue to reflect on my journey thus far, I say, "Hats off, Dad." You were the greatest father, provider, Christian leader of our home, and entrepreneur. I am my father's daughter. I am that apple that fell from my dad's tree. The entrepreneurial legacy that my father modeled before me propelled me into the female entrepreneur I am today. Thanks, Dad, for all that you poured into me and allowed me to see. Some people show you what not to do while others demonstrate exactly what to do.

It's been 10 years since my father passed. His presence is missed greatly; however, his mark and influence on my life and my family's lives live on—so much so that I married "my father." What do I mean by that? God saw fit to give me such an amazing dad that I would not settle for just any man entering my life as a potential husband and life partner. My husband, Mr. Christopher Fitzgerald Pinkney, a great man in his own right, is so much like my dad—hard working, God fearing, consistent, reliable, dependable, and on time.

I was raised by a great man. I watched a great man love my mom, so I would not dare entertain a mate that did not meet those standards. The one thing I am saddened by is the fact that my dad never met my husband. These two men would have hit it off wonderfully. Despite this not happening, God has let me know that he has sanctioned, ordained, and commanded me to begin this next chapter with my husband. The mantle has been passed; I am in good hands.

Today, I have been in business for 24 years, just about half the time my dad ran his. My prayer is that God will continue to guide and lead me in my endeavors as a business owner and now author and all other undertakings He has predestined for me. I have a growing organization that is thriving. In August 2020, our business hit a major milestone, earning a highly prestigious level within our company called The Power Builder Ring (PBR), which includes a major income growth marker. This is just the beginning. Many more PBR earners and diamond jumpers will come from my organization.

The sign of a true leader is not just settling for what happens to you but recognizing what you can help make happen for others. New leadership emerges daily within my organization, and my mission is to be an entrepreneurial example for many people that I lead and mentor (paying it forward). I am the head of a female-owned business with many women following me. Together we will continue to *break the rules*. (Shout out to the men on our team. Coach loves you too). As a woman-led organization and a proud African-American woman, I was born to break the rules, born to set new trends, to carry on the legacy of my father and raise the torch for financial freedom.

I will remain young and ambitious. (This is a state of mind, not an age). I will remain female and competitive, and I will continue to be the apple that fell from my dad's tree aka "Daddy's little girl." This little girl is all grown up now, ready to break every rule that has held a woman back, made her feel less than, unworthy, or ill equipped. The devil is a liar. I am every woman, I am somebody, I am a rulebreaker and a barrier buster. How about you?

MARILYN

"Come to the edge," he said.
"We can't, we're afraid!" they responded.
"Come to the edge," he said.
"We can't, We will fall!" they responded.
"Come to the edge," he said.
And so they came.
And he pushed them.
And they flew.

—Guillaume Apollinaire

In our culture, what isn't a rule or some predetermined norm or suggestion from another person that becomes the standard established precept? Sometimes it is hard to tell the difference between a rule and an accepted norm. It's equally difficult to find yourself on the outside of a "rule" as you internally struggle for what makes sense to you about you.

So many issues can potentially arise when we seek to discover what fits for our lives. We may find ourselves saying, "Is that your way or mine; I don't live that way; my process is not like yours; I parent differently; I wear another style of clothing." In essence, when you allow the daylight to come, you realize that much of what you've been taught are someone else's rules, which may not align with your own truths. Ah, peace! Now what do you do with that realization?

At this point in my life and my career, when I look back, I wonder what took me so long to stop being controlled by other people's rules and ideas of what my life should look like. These rules now guide me to take a pause, listen, evaluate, and check in with a moment of silence to discern my desire, to ask my heartbeat what I want without allowing these rules to control me.

All around us, society and individuals reflect back different opinions about everything from politics to the way to bring up a child. Other people want to tell us how to work and how to live. Chances are many aspects of our lives have rules imposed by someone else. Because these rules are forced upon us from the outside, they may feel like a mountain to climb.

I am reminded on a regular basis how easy it is to shift back into someone else's box, to slip into a remembered pattern that feels like a chasm. Since memories are stored, that is not a difficult concept to comprehend.

Here's an example from my life. What am I reminded of when I see a maroon-colored anything—even a maroon car? When I was a little girl, maybe five or six, I remember going to my grandparents' home for a visit every week. My grandparents did not speak much English, so upon arrival my brother and I sat on their maroon-colored velour sofa like little dolls. The sofa was the softest thing I can remember. I would curl up in a corner and, before I knew it, I was asleep. At my grandparents' house, there was no playing outside, no special food, and not much TV. No fun for a kid. I usually felt sad and didn't want to go.

You probably can guess one outcome of the maroon-colored sofa experience? I don't like maroon. Even though the sofa was soft and yummy, which I loved, the dislike was far more powerful and won that contest. Thus, my rule came to life: Maroon is just not my color. Poor little maroon really didn't hurt me, but the mere association ruined my relationship with the color for life, sort of. I can break free from most of the disdain, of course, if it really matters. I might always retain some remnants though.

What about those issues that we are unaware of? Certain life experiences leave an everlasting impression, molding our very existence, establishing boundaries and rules when we don't realize they live inside us.

My parents were strong and opinionated. They gave me my way many times, but that freedom did not come devoid of strong opinions that nullified and weakened mine. When I chose to ignore the outcome of their spurn and do anything my way, it required internal strength. It represented a personal triumph. Do you remember getting ready to jump into a pool of frigid water and sucking in because you knew it would be so, so cold? Well, that's how it felt to do my own thing. Squeeze in, avoid the pain, the fear, the repercussions, and jump in *my way*. Diving in actually worked out in my favor, and in a minute I will tell you why.

My mother, now 94, was and is the queen of the kitchen. She did not work outside our home and the kitchen was her domain. Do you think that might be why cooking is *not* my thing and why I focused on the business world? Putting two and two together and with what you have learned about me so far, knowing my parents were strong, and I had my fights, you can see why I left the kitchen out of my repertoire. My mother never needed help in her queendom. If by chance I slid in a chore, she usually did it better by correcting me. Her way became the only way.

Can I let you in on a little secret? It is the same way today. She really is a fabulous cook, and the kitchen remains her territory. We all can use at least one area of expertise, a place that represents our domain. I appreciate that she has this. Now, let's combine my mother's crown in the kitchen with my parents' overall clout, as I saw it, and say they ruled. The carrot was there, but I couldn't eat it. I don't think it was even dangling. The fear of being wrong and not sizing up did not bode well for my beginning. Okay, but I told you it worked out in my favor, right?

That leads me to this moment in my history and my journey through a garden full of someone else's laws to where I found my golden rules. All rules were made to be broken, I realized! And I did. I love whoever said that. Did they make that statement just for me? Nah, I think they said it for you too. When it comes to my own favorite standby quote discovered by guess who, I often hear myself repeating, "Whose fear am I fearing anyway?!" My answer, needless to say, is to look deep within by taking a snapshot of the fear while finding my truth. This happens in slow motion, freezing the frame and giving me a timeless moment. Once I dissect the fear and my response,

I realize I don't own that cumbersome fear or stress. I am free from its shackles and can continue on to my rebirth. My guidance stands like a fortress and I go forth. Ahh.

I took the feelings of inadequacies and hurled myself through the fear, through the fire, and found my solid ground with a kidlike sense of fun, adventure, and a core that said, "Why not?! What ya got to lose?" And with some humor, I lose someone else's North Star, making room for my own.

You know how they say it's not the big stresses that will kill you but the little ones over time that will be the deadly destroyer? It is actually the ones you are not keyed into, that you are unaware of that will get you. Well, hear this: It's those tiny stressors laced with fear that gnaw at your soul, personality, energy, your unique vibe, essence, and your will to live. Rules are stressful when they don't belong to you and you are trying to make them fit like your old comfortable shoe. Those hidden fears become your truth and your very reason for being, the soup you suffer in, and they surely will drag you down and shorten your life by the misery they cause.

Breaking rules is the only way to make your mark in the sand and defeat those fatal fears. Create your own path and decorate it with big, juicy, sparkly puff paint. Making your imprint colorful and large allows you to rise above the fabric of perception ever so slightly. Then, when you are ready to break the next rule, you add more and more paint for a different, bolder look.

Your life, your rules, are your choice. The world actually needs you to break the mold that keeps you inside the box of limitation, inhibited by the rules that were thrust upon you. We need your specialness, creativity, emotion, authenticity, and truth.

Do you have some shtick or personal routine or message that you tell yourself and others to believe about you? If we were in a classroom, I would be raising my hand, saying, "I do; I do." Well, I did. For years, I told myself I could not write, my spelling sucked, and I had no talent. I remember when I taught special education for a year, at the time it felt like the worst year of my life and career. The educational system had too many rules and conflicts. Like an unhappy child, every day I woke up to go to school feeling sick to my stomach. I have always had a difficult time surviving in a system that doesn't make sense, and to me the educational system didn't. As I drove to school each day, over and over I asked myself, "What is my talent? I can't sing, dance, draw, or write. What is my art?" I struggled feeling like a loser without an artistic gift that belonged to me—something unique to me, full of self-expression. On one of those trips to school, I discovered my talent: my mouth, my comfort zone. I was good at talking, persuading people, sharing information, and making presentations. But I have to say I wasn't satisfied. Could my mouth actually be an art form? My quick answer: it didn't represent the art box I was accustomed to seeing. I wanted more. I love art and creativity. Whether in an art gallery, around music, amongst artists, or in conversation about art, I felt at home in the art world. I wanted to be able to articulate art, but it was where I had the least amount of self-confidence. It didn't matter that I loved it and felt a kindred spirit connection; my confidence wasn't there.

So, I accepted my mouth as my art, but I wasn't satisfied. I opposed it as my only art. I had to become a writer, an author. I set out to break the shtick rule about writing I imagined I felt. Collapsing a rule should come with some bad feelings, right? Not as bad as perpetuating that rule, I discovered. Along I went. Pulling my hair out with my hands became my constant occupation as I sat at my computer writing my first book. I struggled and struggled, swaying in my seat like I was on a fishing boat in a storm. I was squirmishing, which is my word for the ultimate in agonizing.

Finally, I did it. It was not easy. I wanted to write more than I wanted to accept that uncomfortable feeling as my own. I believed those sensations belonged to someone else. How could they be mine? How could any insecurity be mine? In the process of writing and squirmishing, the ecstasy of finding new ways of saying something, being able to express a feeling in a way that was spot on, far outweighed the sea sickness. My mission as a writer was to tell the stories of marginal populations whose words and lives may never meet the ears and eyes of their neighbors, colleagues, and tribe without a book. The possibility that these stories could chip away at our society's perceived differences, removing the stain of ignorance, carried me through my challenges. A second book, *In Just One Afternoon: Listening Into the Hearts of Twins*, and many more mistakes later, I came closer to experiencing a glimmer of joy for the discoveries seen through the heart of twins. Ah, then, voila, the third book! I began loving what I wrote or, as I often say, what came through me. Now, I have finished the fourth book, and I'm there. Faith abounds and I now know I can write. No, I am not a Nobel prize winner or a *New York Times* bestselling author yet, but I am further along than I thought, and I don't need the *New York Times'* list to validate my work. Nope, I don't. No one knows the confidence stream I feel that oozes out from me, flowing back and forth within like the tide that comes, stronger and stronger, at the beginning and end of each day. I am that confident regardless of some list. It's the self-assurance I take with me everywhere. Not used to saying it yet, I still shudder when I tell people I am an author, but I say it anyway. Leftover yuck. However, I don't care if it's unformattable. I enter my out-of-body experience, acknowledging myself as an author to myself, and I go with it. One day I will hear something, and I will know.

Rules are fickle and, when met head on, melt away like the witch in *The Wizard of Oz* or any bully. They become an entity only when we give them substance and form. Creative ideas float in the ethers of the collective consciousness, seeking a fertile place to land. Let the universe know you will provide a welcome environment for them to be born.

Guess what happens when you don't let those ideas in? They find someone else who will. Ideas are an entity whose time has come. They want to become form and substance. Don't allow a rule to stand in the way of this force that wants so much for you to be its best friend. Give yourself the chance to step into the fire and ice. I have done a lot of dancing in the flames and diving into the ice—sometimes more fire than ice and other times more ice than fire, but in the end it's my life, my choice. I don't see any option.

Besides being an author (see, I said it), I have a coaching practice. Thankfully, I got past the dialogue with myself that asked who am I to work with and advise people. Who am I *not* to? I host a live online TV talk show each week, which takes a lot of chutzpah even after nine years. Here I focus on the good I am doing by sharing great stories. I am told that, and I listen. I am the founder of Women's Power Networking and our women challenge me regularly. I am leading a global community of homeopaths, which I am taking care of for a friend. I didn't know much about homeopathy, but I do know business. Laughing about how I find myself in uncertain situations is my normal way of embracing a new experience.

Guess what? Women are blazing trails and are throwing you a lifeline. Take it and pay the line forward. Toss the line back like a bouquet and just imagine the possibilities.

The awareness of hardened rules did not arise on the day we were born. Both the rules and our response to them came later with experience and learning. Test your constitution and see what actually awaits you. Watch as your noes, can'ts, shouldn'ts, avoids, denials, not me's and blocks turn into curiosity, into so whats, maybes, miracles, humor, smiles, into "Wow, that is me?" and into who knows what else. The door is open. Pass through it to your own wonderment and squeeze in if necessary. Break those rules and let's clear the path for each other. What is waiting for you?

MARTY

THERE IS LIFE AFTER RETIREMENT

Let me start out by confessing that I'm retired. So how does my story fit in this book about women who break rules to succeed in their own businesses? Well, my retirement doesn't look like what might come to mind when you hear the word "retired." You may imagine someone slowing down to take a well-deserved rest from the rat race or traveling, spending time with the grandkids, finally getting around to all those long-overdue home projects, you know, enjoying some leisure time. I enjoy doing those things too. But I've always dreamed of having my own business. I didn't know what it would be. I just knew I wanted one. So, at age 64, I decided to break some rules, jump the corporate ship, and begin a new life. How this all came about, though, was a lifetime in the making.

I guess I've always been a rulebreaker without knowing it. When I was young, my parents allowed me to be creative and follow my dreams. I spent hours in my father's workshop building things from scraps of wood or other leftover materials.

In high school, home economics opened up a whole new world to me: sewing. Fashion design sparked my imagination, and I began creating most of my wardrobe. I started with easy projects like A-line skirts and simple dresses. Then, without giving a thought about whether I was experienced enough, I went on to tackle bathing suits, coats, and evening gowns. One of my favorites was the red moire gown with ruffled neckline that I wore to my high school Christmas formal. I even made my own white satin and lace wedding gown, complete with detachable train.

Music and theater were an important part of my life. When I was in my single digits, I put on plays and shows with the kids in my neighborhood. This led to my involvement in creating costumes for my town's Children's Theater as a teen.

91

I played guitar in an all-girl rock band (not too many of those in the mid-60s). I started a music club with some of my friends and we ran local teen dances. More rules ignored. Imagine a group of 16 and 17-year-olds planning and running a dance in a local hall without any adult supervision!

I didn't think twice about being able to do these things because no one ever told me I couldn't, so I was oblivious to the rules. Failure and limitations weren't words in my vocabulary.

Music and creativity are in my blood. My father was a trumpet player. In the 40s and 50s, he played in big bands and marched in parades with the Marine Bugle Corps. My mother grew up with five siblings on a farm in Sandy Hook, Connecticut. Farm life was hard and money was scarce, but her mother, my grandmother, saw Mom's musical potential. She traded house cleaning services so my mom could take singing lessons. Mom became an accomplished soprano, singing in local bands and church choirs. I still get chills remembering Mom's operatic voice as she sang "O Holy Night" and "Ave Maria," two of her favorites. Now, struggling with vascular dementia at 91 years old, she still remembers songs from her childhood. It's bittersweet to hear her break into song with a much weaker voice or to learn how her singing entertained her caregivers at the assisted living facility.

Music even played a part in my parents' first encounter. My dad met my mom at the Pleasure Beach Ballroom and asked her to dance. That was the spark that ignited their 50-plus year marriage. They always made a very attractive couple, Dad with his curly dark hair and Mom with her movie-star looks.

My Dad was a "hands on" person. He repaired and renovated everything in our house. Woodworking was his specialty. I fondly remember him building a laundry chute on the main floor so Mom wouldn't have to lug laundry down to the basement. Dad also loved to draw. When he retired he funneled his creative talents into a wood craft business. I could always find him in the basement working on some new project. He enlisted Mom to paint his creations. The two of them were known as "The Cellar Dwellers" at local craft fairs where they sold their treasures. In a way my parents broke some of the traditional rules in their earlier and later years by embracing their creativity. This was the environment that nurtured me in childhood and beyond.

This isn't to say I grew up totally without rules. I am the oldest of four children, and there is a seven-year gap between me and my next sibling. For the first seven years of my life, I was an only child. It was great to have all the attention, but I also had all the focus. If I misbehaved, there was no getting around it. On the other hand, being the oldest and being mostly around adults early on, I was treated as if I were more mature. And I guess I was. But that led me to feel like I had to live up to that maturity level and please everyone. And being a people pleaser meant behaving perfectly. Perfectionism became a way of life.

Rules prevailed in the strict Catholic elementary school I attended from second to eighth grade. The nuns had no qualms about using the 12-inch rulers hidden in the sleeves of their habits to crack some knuckles if anyone in our class of 50 students got even a little out of hand. I remember being in a row of girls who all had their backs smacked because we weren't singing loudly enough. Maybe this was crowd control? After all, there were 50 of us to one nun!

When I finally broke out of Catholic school after eighth grade graduation and moved on to public high school, I was amazed at the freedom my fellow classmates enjoyed. We were allowed to express our opinions and encouraged to be creative. We had choices in the classes we elected. There were opportunities to discover our talents in the arts.

Of course, there still were rules. But they weren't the stern commandments of my elementary school experience, obeyed to avoid the harsh consequences of noncompliance. This experience left its mark. I became timid because of it, and my shyness held me back from doing things I wanted to do. I remember opting out of a high school theater arts class I was so excited to be in, only a few days after the class started. I felt intimidated by the other students in the class whom I saw as more talented and confident than me.

I tentatively navigated between being reserved and being outgoing in my high school classes, depending on the level of teacher encouragement and class camaraderie. But all in all I flourished during my high school years while keeping a relatively low profile. And I met the love of my life when I was 16 at a Catholic Youth Organization event. So, from a teenage perspective, all was good.

Enter adulthood! High school graduation loomed. I dreamed of going to fashion design school in New York City. But reality crashed in. There was no way my parents could come up with the tuition for college. And I was in a serious relationship with my soon-to-be husband (the same love of my life from high school), so a higher education was not in the cards.

The rules started trickling in. When I graduated from high school, my parents were adamant that I find a job with medical benefits. They wanted to spare me the financial hardship they were going through. My father was a hard-working physical laborer for his uncle's building moving company. Yes, they actually moved buildings, mostly residential houses in the construction path of Interstate 95. It was fascinating work, but it was also low paying with no medical insurance. Mom's full-time job was raising me and my three younger siblings, who were always coming down with colds, strep throat, and ear infections. Medical and household expenses drained their limited income, so it was understandable that they insisted I find a full-time job with good pay and benefits. Without a college degree, creative jobs provided neither. I became shackled by the responsibility of making a living in the "real world." Reluctantly, I gave up my job at JoAnn Fabrics (as it was called then) to begin clerical work in Bridgeport Hospital's Social Services Department. My self-expression, creativity, and dreams lingered in the background.

I married my soulmate on October 10, 1970, 16 months after my high school graduation, at the tender age of 19. He was just a few months shy of 23. The Vietnam War was in full force during the early years of our marriage. We survived the threat of my husband's repeated Army draft notices and subsequent medical exemption appeals for hypertension. We also overcame his time away from home as he worked full time and spent nights continuing his college education. We were overjoyed when I became pregnant with our first child, but the joy was short-lived when the pregnancy ended in miscarriage in the third month.

I left my job at the hospital shortly after I became pregnant, so now I was a full-time housewife. I loved being the boss of my agenda, taking care of our apartment and having time to sew. And it wasn't long before I was pregnant again. We welcomed our daughter Tracey in April 1973.

In January 1979, the three of us moved to the four-bedroom colonial we had built in a new neighborhood in Shelton, Connecticut. You know what they say: new house, new baby. Cheryl made her entrance in October 1979. And Lauren followed four years later in January 1983. Our family was now complete with three daughters, each four grades apart in school!

The years of being a stay-at-home mom were challenging but fulfilling. My girls were eager to have me involved in their activities: Brownies, Girl Scouts, dancing school, soccer, and all their school and church events. I used my sewing and craft talents whenever I could, making their clothes, Halloween costumes, and various craft projects. As the girls grew, I devoted more time to exercise and joined a local aerobics class. I enjoyed it so much I became certified by my instructor and started teaching classes at her aerobics studio. This was the Jane Fonda sweatbands and matching leg warmers era. The Pointer Sisters' "Jump" was a class favorite as were songs from *Top Gun* and *Dirty Dancing*. I loved mixing my class playlists and choreographing movements to inspire the women in my classes to have fun and enjoy exercise.

When Lauren, my youngest, started first grade, my three girls were finally all in school full time. My husband and I talked about my returning to work part time, just to earn an extra hundred dollars a week. I hadn't worked since the 70s and offices were much more advanced than they were back then. I was going from electric typewriters, Dictaphones, and mimeograph machines to computers, copiers, and fax machines. I sharpened my typing skills on our home computer and scoured the newspaper classified ads for a part-time secretarial position. I applied for one company that was located close to my parents' home, and my mom agreed to babysit if one of the girls got sick. Surprisingly, I got the job! Looking back on it, I see how unprepared I was to reenter the job market. I guess that was another broken rule—I leaped before I looked! But I was a quick learner and my coworkers were patient mentors. My confidence grew with each new accomplishment. This was the first of many part-time jobs I held over the next decade. Every one added tools to my skill set and broadened my experience.

When my girls were in high school and college, I decided the time was right to shift into full-time employment. I signed on with an employment agency and took advantage of their free computer training while I searched for a job.

One day while I was busy learning Excel at the agency, they approached me with a temp job offer for a company in the same building. The catch was I had to start immediately. Again, leaping before looking, I took them up on it. I joke that my family might have feared I was kidnapped if they were looking for me, because they had no idea I had started a job that day.

That was the beginning of my full-time employment. The temp job was in the Finance Department, but I was poached by the Human Resources Director and offered a permanent position. He was the first of my two most empowering bosses. He encouraged me to enroll in a Human Resources certification program at a local university. This was an exhilarating yet intimidating experience for me. I had no college background and was probably the oldest student in my classes. But I was excited to learn business communication, organizational management, and employment law in a field I was coming to love. And I made the dean's list with a 3.95 average! I now felt I found my niche in Human Resources (HR). What started out as a job was evolving into a career.

When the company downsized and I was laid off, I landed another HR position in the corporate office of a company in New Canaan, Connecticut. Again, I was fortunate to work for an empowering boss who mentored me and was always open to my ideas. If our opinions differed, he would say, "Convince me." Sometimes I was able to persuade him and sometimes not, but it always led to lively discussions and fair resolutions. With him as my advocate, I worked my way up the ranks to become the manager of employee health and welfare benefits. This opened up more formal learning opportunities in the Certified Employee Benefits Specialists (CEBS) certification program. I successfully passed the exams of the first two courses. My job also involved travel to the company's U.S. plants, presenting programs and attending seminars and workshops. Every new responsibility increased my expertise and bolstered my confidence.

It also fueled my passion for learning and self-improvement. I discovered that I embrace change that leads to growth, progress, and positive transformation.

My biggest personal transformation came the year I turned 60. I was forced to accept the truth. My husband's drinking was an uncontrollable disease. His detox, month-long rehabilitation, and AA meetings only delayed the inevitable. He relapsed into drinking and emotional abuse. Our 40-year marriage was failing. My home was no longer the haven I desperately needed after long, demanding hours at work. I felt like I was leaving one stressful situation for another. I needed to escape. My birthday is close to the 4th of July, so in retrospect I declared my 60th as Independence Day.

I repeatedly demanded that my husband move out of our home to no avail. When I came home from work he was still there, refusing to budge. I realized if I wanted a separation, I was the one who had to leave. I found and moved to a two-bedroom apartment in New Canaan within walking distance to my office. Another rule broken: "in sickness and in health…till death do us part."

Ironically, my husband died six months after I left, and I became a widow. I was at work when my husband's brother called to tell me. The news felt like someone had punched me in the back. My heart broke for my children who lost their once loving father to alcoholism. But I lost my husband years before his actual death. I had done my grieving as our relationship fell apart. To me his death was the end of a chapter and a relief. He passed before we started an expensive divorce process. I ended up in a much better financial place. Sometimes I shock people by saying he did me a favor by dying. It may be a callous statement, but it was truly how I felt!

Before I separated from my husband, I took on most of the household responsibilities because his illness prevented him from doing many of the things he used to do. But now as a widow I was responsible for everything, and it was overwhelming. Still, I buried my feelings and forced myself to pick up the pieces to get my life back on track. I was afraid that if I gave in to the overwhelm, panic would push me over the edge.

There were many challenges and lots of hard physical work. The home my husband and I had shared for over 30 years had accumulated a lifetime of family possessions. It took over a year of weekends to sort through them, deciding what to keep and what to sell. Then came the renovations, cleaning and staging to prep my house for sale. I interviewed realtors and analyzed neighborhood comps. Rule followed. I finally settled on a price that was disappointingly lower than I thought the house was worth. But before I could sign a contract with an agency, fate stepped in. A contractor who was working on my house made an offer to buy it. We negotiated a price that was higher than the realtors' intended asking price. I couldn't believe it! I never thought I could sell a house on my own, and now I was doing it. Not only was I getting more money for my house, but I was also circumventing realtor commissions! Rule broken.

With the house sold, I settled into single life. One thing I learned about becoming single for the first time in decades was the impact it had on my social life. I was no longer half of a couple, so invitations from my couple friends stopped coming. Distance played a part too. My apartment was 25 miles away from my former home. It was less convenient for my friends and family to visit. I found myself doing most of the traveling if I wanted to hang out with them. It was lonely and I often felt isolated.

But being single had its advantages. It gave me the opportunity to live my life in a way that expressed who I am. I didn't realize how restricted and unhappy I was until the day I left my husband. Now I reveled in my new freedom. I loved decorating my apartment and entertaining, especially cooking and trying new recipes. Christmas has always been my favorite time of year, and this year my creativity was in full force. I spread holiday cheer throughout my new home. Snow-flakes, ornaments, pine branches, and decorations were everywhere. My Christmas village display and a decked-out tree completed the scene. I celebrated by hosting a luncheon for my girlfriends. We feasted on comfort food—homemade soups, crusty bread, wine and cheese. Then we bundled up and strolled through downtown New Canaan to window shop and get in the holiday spirit. That year I also invited my coworkers to an after-Christmas potluck party to share camaraderie and our holiday leftovers.

I loved the challenges of my job in Human Resources. As the Health and Welfare Benefits Manager, I had many opportunities to help our employees resolve their insurance issues. Troubleshooting was my specialty. And when my responsibilities shifted in the direction of employee wellness, I was thrilled. Health and wellness have always sparked joy in me. So co-founding the company's first employee wellness program was a challenge I couldn't resist. But I was also apprehensive. This was definitely out of my comfort zone. I felt the imposter syndrome creeping in. Here I was working with the VP of Safety and Health and with plant managers, writing proposals for executives—things I had never done before. It was a huge learning curve to overcome. But again no one ever told me I couldn't, so I pushed myself forward. The pieces of my life were falling into place and I felt fulfilled and triumphant!

Life has a funny way of evolving though. My company was gradually being taken over by its parent company. There were changes in upper management, policies, procedures, and culture. Some of these changes were for the better, but many more were for the worse. I realized it was time I made some changes myself.

Through my involvement in employee wellness, I discovered an emerging field, health coaching. My heart immediately knew this was where I needed to be. I enrolled in a year-long holistic health coach certification program and spent every non-working moment immersed in the fascinating world of wellbeing.

As a life-long learner, I've always loved and respected books. Of all the birthday gifts I've received over the years, one of my favorites was a Nancy Drew book from a friend when I was eight or nine. Books that introduced new ideas and learning experiences were special to me. My parents surprised me with a set of encyclopedias for Christmas one year and I poured into them!

So it was no surprise that I soaked up the material from my certification program, enjoying every moment. But could I actually make a career out of it? I knew I had to trust myself to find out and move ahead. I started making plans to begin the next stage of my life, retiring from my job and establishing my own business. Retiring at 64? Another rule broken.

I always dreamed I would end up in North Carolina. I had visited my two daughters who lived there with their husbands and I fell in love with the area. And my oldest daughter had just given birth to my first (and only) grandchild, a beautiful baby girl! My mind was made up. This is where I was meant to be.

My decision started an exciting but stress filled period of my life. I vowed to keep my retirement plans a secret from people at work until my move was in its final stages. I felt like a secret agent as I traveled back and forth to North Carolina to look for a place to live. I finally decided to build a house in a new subdivision. It had more square footage than the one I sold in Shelton, so I broke the "downsize when you get older" rule! Planning the home design resulted in more trips to North Carolina. My co-workers thought I was such a wonderful grandmother, making so many trips to visit my granddaughter. Little did they know that was only part of the reason!

Juggling the responsibilities of work, school, helping my mom, and moving were physically and emotionally draining. Then I had my "aha" moment! I put a name to the emotions I was struggling with: *stress.* And I knew I wasn't alone. We all are accumulating so much stress. In my studies I learned that stress has a negative impact on our mental, emotional and physical health. It affected my health with weight gain, high cholesterol, pre-diabetes and a non-alcoholic fatty liver. I was shocked to discover that stress is the primary reason for almost 80% of doctor visits. Yet, most patients aren't given effective tools to deal with it. I wasn't. Instead, I was prescribed statins to treat my high cholesterol, which I resisted taking because of the negative side effects.

Doctors treat the symptoms of stress: depression, anxiety, high cholesterol, hypertension, type 2 diabetes, cardiac issues, cancer, and more. But many fail to drill down to find and resolve the sources. Becoming aware of the implications of this, I decided to make stress management the cornerstone of my health coaching practice. I wanted to help others mitigate their stress by identifying it and getting to the root of it. I wanted to share the tools that worked for me. And I wanted to gather as much ammunition as I could to help myself and others fight the stress battle.

I had the passion, but I didn't know the first thing about starting a business, especially in North Carolina. Networking and advice from other small business owners helped. I attended classes offered by local community colleges and business organizations. I enrolled in advanced coaching courses in an attempt to learn all I could. But I was almost paralyzed by the belief that I didn't know enough to be successful. Imposter syndrome again.

Then there were the personal challenges that diverted me from developing my business. My mom's health deteriorated and I helped her move to an assisted living facility in Connecticut. I traveled back and forth from North Carolina to get Mom's house, my childhood home, ready to sell. A few years later, I brought Mom to live in North Carolina. She's been in two different assisted living facilities since she's been in North Carolina, and I've moved her both times. My oldest daughter went through a long difficult divorce. She and my granddaughter moved in with me for a few years as she was getting her life back together. I put my business on hold and made the decision to make my family a priority until my life was more stable.

As my personal responsibilities eased up, I devoted time to do some serious soul searching. I needed to rediscover my purpose and uncover my authentic self. I made the difficult decision to walk away from a group business venture I had been working on. The project was a great learning experience, and I enjoyed collaborating with wellness practitioners like myself. Unfortunately, the project didn't develop into the thriving business I hoped it would. And it was taking my time and energy away from my own business. Loyalty rule broken?

Letting go of things that were not serving me was a scary but freeing experience. After I finally convinced myself that it was okay to let go, it felt like a huge burden was lifted off my shoulders. I was as light as a feather, a bird ready to soar!

With renewed energy, I threw myself into my business. Again, I looked for outside advice. There were so many courses guaranteed to make my business succeed, and I took part in them all. I followed the rules they were spouting. Some were constructive. But some rules didn't resonate with me. I felt uneasy using them. I questioned myself. Wasn't I supposed to push myself out of my comfort zone? Sometimes, yes. But I knew in my heart that not all the rules were right for me. How could I be my authentic self if I didn't believe in what I was doing?

Now, there's nothing wrong with rules per se. Rules control chaos. Rules foster organization. Rules set boundaries. But some boundaries are meant to be overcome.

For a long while, being a perfectionist kept me a prisoner of the rules. I had to do things exactly right. That meant following the rules. Rules set the bar I had to measure up to. If something wasn't absolutely perfect, I would get that queasy feeling in my stomach and be deeply disappointed in myself. Sometimes I put much more effort into achieving perfection than the task was worth. But I didn't recognize that at the time.

Now I realize that not all rules are written in stone. Some are only guidelines, well-meaning advice to help me lead a more orderly life. I'm sure we all agree that we need laws and regulations to govern us as a community, organization, and country. But aren't some rules arbitrary? And who made up these rules anyway? People just like you and me. Did these "experts" have the qualifications to create the rules? Shouldn't we be the experts of ourselves? After all, we've known ourselves all our lives. Following the rules may be the best choice when we don't want or need to reinvent the wheel. But there are times when we should think for ourselves and step outside the box, change the rules to express our individuality, or create a new set of rules that embraces who we are.

Before I retired I dreamed of a time when I wouldn't have to follow certain rules. Rules like getting up early five days a week and working long hours to make someone else's dreams come true. Now in my late 60s, I realize it's time I give myself permission to have that life. You *can* teach an old dog new tricks! Sure, I want my health coaching practice to grow but not at the sacrifice of family time and my own well-being. I choose professional and personal commitments by the value they add to my business and my life. I stopped doing things simply out of obligation, things I used to feel I had to do. Life is too short. But it takes practice. I have to keep reminding myself because it can be so easy to slip back into 60-year-old habits.

I carry these principles into my health coaching practice. My life experiences resonate with clients who struggle with the same situations—women dealing with marital issues, alcoholic spouses, emotional abuse, and widowhood, women entrepreneurs, women who work in the corporate world, women in the sandwich generation, caring for both elderly parents and children/grandchildren. They identify with me because they know I've been there too, and, although the journey isn't over, I'm surviving. And thriving!

I firmly believe everyone has the answers to their problems buried deep within themselves. As a coach I help unearth those answers and guide my clients towards solutions. I'm an accountability partner and a cheerleader. I help analyze challenges, celebrate wins, and everything in between.

Together my clients and I explore the stress of major life-changing events like divorce, separation, death, or loss of a job. But we also identify the daily stress that affects their lives. Most people understand that emotions like worry, anxiety, fear, and anger produce stress. But the feelings caused by inconveniences, interruptions, and frustrations are often overlooked. These accumulating emotions have catastrophic effects on physical and mental health. I help my clients master their stress using the very same tools I use—health coaching strategies that address the whole person as a unique individual.

My favorite stress management tool is the HeartMath® System. Because of its effectiveness, I highly recommend it to my clients and use it as part of my own personal daily practice. HeartMath's mission is to help people align their minds, bodies, and emotions with the intuitive guidance of their hearts. It uses simple yet effective techniques to help people build their resilience to stress and move into an optimal state of functioning known as psychophysiological coherence. Heart-Math® helps to control emotions with self-regulation. It increases energy and improves mental focus to make better decisions, decrease brain fog, and heighten productivity.

I discovered HeartMath® as I was preparing a stress management presentation for my company's engineering department. Their director asked me to speak about managing stress at their annual conference in Albuquerque, New Mexico, because he noticed an increase in physical health issues among the employees in his department. He suspected their physical symptoms were signs of the high level of stress they were experiencing at work. I only like to recommend something that I've actually tried myself, so I tested the HeartMath® techniques before my presentation. After just a few days of practicing the techniques, I noticed a dramatic improvement in my work focus, productivity, energy, and stress level. I was convinced! I became a HeartMath® Certified Coach, and I've added this science-based program to my practice.

My health coaching practice is reconnecting me to my creative side. I express myself through writing and combining art with technology in my social media and other communications. I nurture my love of teaching with in-person and virtual workshops and presentations. And I enjoy troubleshooting to solve problems, remove barriers, and reach my clients' and my own goals.

I strongly believe that things happen for a reason. Each individual life event is like a tiny piece of a one-million-piece puzzle. In the end the jig-sawed bits all fit together to make an awe-inspiring work of art, section by section. Now I see how the episodes in my life, especially the ones that baffled me at the time, fell into place to fulfill a master plan—to get me where I am today and will continue to go.

The coronavirus pandemic has been another dramatic piece of the puzzle. As it has for practically everyone, it's challenged me to redirect the scope of my business and life. Suffering through learning curves of adapting to the virtual world has opened up many new opportunities. Online meetings, presentations, and webinars have broadened my presence to a much wider audience than I had ever imagined. I'm no longer restricted by local, in-person constraints. I do miss the face-to-face contact and will offer some in-person events when the time is right. But now I'm excited to have the ability to reach so many more people with my message. The possibilities are endless if we are willing to change, be flexible, and break some rules!

So my retirement hasn't led to the end of my life's journey—not by a long shot. I see my retirement as a door that opened to a new exciting phase of life, full of promise and opportunity. I've learned that life shouldn't be restricted by the accepted "norm" or limited by status quo—the *rules*! A vibrant life isn't stagnant or bound by rules. It's bursting with purpose and vitality. That's how I intend to live mine. Because no one ever told me I couldn't!

KRISTI W.

"NORMAL" IS NOT ALWAYS NORMAL!

When wading through the muck, don't sit down; strap on your big girl boots and keep going!

I never imagined that I'd wake up on a cool concrete sidewalk one sunny Saturday afternoon in a busy public park. How could one get *there*? As I started to come around, I remember vaguely hearing the birds chirping, feeling the warm sun on my face, and hearing my two young children, ages five and two, laughing and playing on the far side of the playground structures. We had just had the most delicious lunch at a nearby bakery. The bread was so soft and the tomato soup warmed us from the inside out. We had hit the park afterwards to work out some energy, or so I thought. This was my last "wake-up call"! Here's my story....

Lying on that hard concrete that day, confused, exhausted and fed up, I decided that enough was enough. I could hardly hold my eyes open.

As an elementary school child, my older brother and I were classic latchkey kids because our parents worked full time in the neighboring town. They were hardworking, nose to the grindstone every day, trying the best way they knew how, to provide for us all the things they didn't have as kids. My mother moved about like a swift animal with many arms, cleaning, cooking, and getting stuff done like there were two of her. My dad was a master of everything outdoors—cars, yard, and anything that needed to be fixed. They both grew up without a lot of extras, like an indoor bathroom when my mother was young. My mother was reared on a farm with two sisters and a brother where they grew or raised most of what they ate and made some of what they wore. Her mother was the boss; she kept everything in line, even all of us grandkids. Her father was a kindhearted man who passed when I

107

was very young. My dad grew up with a brother and sister in a small town nearby. His father was a small business owner, and his mother was the sweetest woman you would ever meet.

Despite only having a high school education, my parents eventually found their way to professional government careers. They were always super focused on working hard so we could have a better life and opportunities they didn't have. As we got older, we naturally were expected to take care of ourselves while they worked. The independence it brought was a blessing (at the time) and a curse (as a reflection).

I remember riding the bus to and from school and having free reign of the house for about three hours every day, which included binge watching TV and eating whatever looked good in the pantry. I loved that part! Now, we didn't have an enormous selection of junk food, but for me ice cream was my best friend. I remember thinking the whole bus ride home about those large vanilla milkshakes with sweetened instant coffee flavors mixed in. My mouth watered as the bus drew closer to the house. Scooping and mixing the perfect milkshake in the biggest cup I could find brought great pleasure. If only I knew then what I know now and how this would be one of many choices that would wreck my health later on. This love affair quickly made me a pudgy fifth grader. I felt upset when I started to notice how I looked in my clothes and beside my friends. At school they would line us up in health class and weigh each person at the beginning of the year, which was an eye opener for me. Luckily, with some growth spurt timing and a hard breakup with ice cream, I shed those extra pounds before middle school. Middle school is tough enough for young people, and I so desperately wanted to feel "pretty." We still had the most colorful cereals in the cabinet, hot toaster strudels, toasted pop tarts with melted butter, and baked cinnamon buns with orange icing drizzled on top for breakfast. My brother and I used to fight over that orange icing.

By high school, I became fascinated with the models on the covers of magazines. Of course, we didn't have smart phones or social media, but there was plenty of influence on TV and the magazine rack at the local grocery store. I read about what they were eating and the exercises they were doing in hopes that maybe I could look like them one day. I even signed up for modeling classes that taught you how to walk and pose for pictures. I thought that maybe one day I would be famous and make tons of money. I found my way to the local YMCA for step classes (remember those). Like so many young people these days, this started my career of dieting and worrying about what my body looked like. There was no internet and the newest fad diet was low fat and no red meat. By that time, I had relinquished the sugary breakfast choices of middle school and opted for slightly less sugary cans of Slimfast for breakfast. I experimented with the grapefruit diet and the cottage cheese diet in the quest for that body I would see on TV. I felt alone, unwilling to share my innermost thoughts with family or close friends.

This obsession continued into college. When I so desperately wanted to lose the freshman 15 that snuck up behind me like a cat, I latched onto the low-fat diet craze, which was another detrimental choice along my health journey. In the early 1990s, it was common to see books and advertisements touting low-fat, higher carb diets. A bagel with low-fat butter was my go-to breakfast in college—yet another example of the choices that stripped my health of its natural superpowers.

My first wake-up call was at dinner one night with my dad who was in town after a business trip. I was so sleepy after my meal that I lay down in the booth across from him while he was eating and wanted to go to sleep. He didn't understand why I was so sleepy and frankly neither did I. This became more common after a meal, and sometimes while driving would need to pull over to wake myself back up again. On school breaks I felt glued to the sofa with no desire to peel myself off and do anything. I kept thinking, *why do I feel so tired? I see other college kids my age playing outside and having fun, but for me it's a chore.* Sure, I could drink coffee to help me get up and go, but why did I feel like such a lazy blob? From my dorm window, I would watch other students play sand volleyball and wish I could go join them. I played volleyball in high school, but I couldn't muster the energy to do it now. I didn't want to feel this way, but my body wasn't cooperating.

When I started to feel more depressed and like the life force had been sucked out of me, I began to seek medical advice. I made appointments with doctor after doctor, but none of them had anything novel to say. Eventually, I stumbled upon one who knew the answer. He was patient and listened carefully. I felt as though he had no other patients in the waiting room.

"You are reactive hypoglycemic," he told me, a blood sugar regulation problem. Of course, I had no idea what this really meant other than I needed to change my diet again. When I did this, I started to feel better, although still not like everyone around me.

What was wrong with me? Did I really feel that different from everyone else, or were they faking it secretly just like me? I was determined not to let it get the best of me, so I got super strict about getting more sleep and lots of exercise, but I continued the same high carb diet just with more fats and caffeine to get me through. This worked pretty well for a few more years, but the damage ensued.

Fast forward through college graduation, career, marriage and two kids. The decline in energy and sharp mental acuity was so gradual that it was unnoticeable for a while. Shortly after my second child was born, my symptoms became impossible to ignore. My gas tank was on empty by dinner, and I slept 11 hours a night without waking up refreshed. I was so drowsy in the afternoons that I would give anything for a nap. This is how I found myself lying on the ground at the park with my kids that afternoon. I just needed to lie down for just a moment to rest my eyes because I couldn't bear to hold them open any longer. I woke up to my husband asking me if I was okay. I was so confused. I thought I had laid down for just a moment, but in reality I slept on the ground for almost an hour. What did the other moms walking by think of me lying there on the sidewalk sleeping?

This was my second wake-up call. I felt like the worst mother, like my kids were getting shortchanged in some way when I had nothing left to give except the remote to watch cartoons. My husband didn't understand why I was always so tired all the time, and frankly neither did I. There was no end in sight. Would my kids grow up and remember their tired, lazy mom, or would my husband finally give up on having a vibrant wife to enjoy life with? I had forgotten the conversations of my original doctor in college who gave me the answer and didn't connect the dots till later.

I scheduled yet another visit with my gynecologist who told me repeatedly year after year that my labs were "normal," and that it was "just motherhood," like I had to accept this new way of life. But I had friends with small children who didn't seem to feel the way I did. I had never felt so utterly alone and frustrated before in my life. I kept asking and searching until eventually I returned to the doctor who gave me the original diagnosis in college. He patiently explained why carbs and sugar were making me feel so depleted. My body was now overreacting due to decades of abuse, to carbs and refined sugars, resulting in a "crash" (sleepy) after I ate them. I finally understood. After hearing this, the "your labs are normal" answer that I got for so many years was starting to really piss me off. I learned what I needed to know to turn things around, but I felt angry at the doctors who had failed me for so long. Why would they dismiss these symptoms in a young new mother as "normal"? There was nothing about what I was feeling that was "normal." They were supposed to know more than me; they were supposed to be my guides. My anger fueled my determination to get well and be that person that my kids and husband needed me to be.

I dove in headfirst, totally revamping my plate, reading labels, and studying menus. I lowered my carbohydrate/fruit/sugar/caffeine intake during the day, and, to my dismay, I stopped falling asleep. Learning about my condition and what I could do to manage it was my new obsession. I could now manage my day without having to sleep after lunch and could stay awake past dinner. I didn't feel so overwhelmed and useless, but it wasn't great yet.

About the same time, by chance, I met an acupuncturist who introduced me to a whole new philosophy of nourishing foods and I fell in love with the Weston A. Price Foundation. This organization was what I had been searching for all those years, a community and a way of eating and healing your body that no one had taught me. I sobbed during our first session because I felt guilty about the carb-heavy foods that I had raised my daughter on for the first three years of her life. Again, I felt I had failed her as a mother. This would be my chance to break the cycle in my own family and ensure that educating her would make a difference in the rest of her life. This time I had to revamp what I fed to my entire family.

No longer would I have to accept empty responses that were given to me by the traditional medical community. I was once told that I was supposed to be tired because I had two small children. Wow, that was original.

Shortly after my son was born, my brain again had stopped working well. I felt like I had ADD; I couldn't concentrate or think clearly. I would sit at my computer and just stare at the screen, trying to figure out what I had sat down to do in the first place. I could get through my day without napping, but I didn't have abundant energy, and it was getting harder to keep up with the kids and the demands of life. It wasn't uncommon to sit down on the sofa at 6:00 p.m. and not want to get up or just stumble into the bed by 9:00p.m. This was no life. I couldn't understand why this kept happening and was running out of patience. Back to the drawing board. For the next couple of years, I searched again for someone who could give me answers.

I stumbled upon a famous biohacker, Dave Asprey, and experimented with his "coffee blended with butter and MCT oil" recommenddation. It sounded so weird and by this time I was hooked on one of the famous coffee chains, which was full of sugar. What did I have to lose, I thought. My ability to function was pretty low at this point, and this coffee magically brought my brain back online. Yet again, I was blown away by the community of people searching for answers like me. I was filled with excitement to be surrounded by like-minded people. As I began to think more clearly and gain back some energy, I researched a new coaching program offered by The Human Potential Institute. Could I actually help others who were in my shoes get their lives back on track? I decided to go for it! I flew to California that October and my path made another turn.

Three months into my training, I was desperate when I noticed that my now 12-year-old had a similar episode of sleepiness after eating. I knew what that was. My personal nightmare just started all over again. I enlisted a local integrative doctor whom I had heard about for several years. Had I failed my child again? I thought I had this figured out. I thought I had taken the steps necessary to protect her from my fate.

This visit marked another turn on my winding path. The integrative doctor explained the biochemistry and we had a plan! She tested my thyroid again, but this time she noted that the lab ranges most doctors follow are too wide and that her narrow range showed that I was under functioning. I could have kissed her! Finally, someone who could see and understand how I felt. I had been dragging day in and out like I was wearing a 50-pound backpack. She got me back on track and diagnosed my daughter with the same issue.

At this point I started to fully appreciate the skills I had acquired over the years of refusing mediocrity and incompetence. I would continue to learn, search, and think outside of the box to find answers to my burning questions. There is a famous book on curiosity and how it reshapes you as a person. I'm not exactly sure when I got bitten by the curiosity bug, but I had *lots* of questions as a child and still do.

Now I was empowered with knowledge that I'd never been exposed to before and had learned how to find answers and refuse ineffectiveness. I will forever be grateful that I began my own personal journey into functional medicine and the benefits of hacking your own biology. In my late 40s, I decided to change my career so that I could empower others in their health journey.

After 12 months of training and certification, I discovered what would be the next major shift in my professional life. I read a book, as I had hundreds of times before, that showed a scientific way to shift imbalances in the brain and revealed that your thyroid is the control center of everything that happens in your body. When my daughter's anxiety began to rear its ugly head, this revelation made perfect sense. I wasn't going to fail at this; there was too much at stake. Again, I dove into nine more months of training to learn how to balance neurotransmitters in the brain.

This training was life changing. The clients I worked with had transformational experiences. It was almost surreal in a way that little ole me could do something so impactful with another struggling person. Now I wanted to share it with the world. I didn't want another person to have to suffer needlessly, but I didn't know how to scale this to reach the number of people that I would have liked to reach.

Yet again, another woman crossed my path and changed the trajectory of my journey. An Australian female entrepreneur who had built and failed over and over in her online businesses had finally figured out how to do it herself and teach others her blueprint. She was affecting the lives of thousands of women, and that's exactly what I was destined to do. I hired her as my business coach and began building a portal of information that could be shared with the world. It felt so exciting to finally see a way to share with so many people the work that I have witnessed change lives and to imagine mitigating pain and suffering. It sounds so cliché, but the helper's high is real, and I found a way to do it on a much larger scale than I ever thought possible. At the same time, I felt petrified. I didn't know anything about cameras and lighting or video editing software, but there's no way I'd let that stop me. This model broke all of the rules of a traditional coaching business, and fortunately I had the technical background to give it a whirl!

Through all of my ups and downs, I learned not to accept "there's nothing you can do" or "everything looks normal" as an answer when I knew deep in the pit of my gut that it was not the right answer. I learned to listen to my intuition, to trust my passion for "why," even if the path seemed impossible and unclear, and to never give up. I don't remember a time since middle school that I felt like skipping and doing cartwheels, but I do now. Someone my age skipping around may look silly at times, but, when you feel like it, you just do it.

I have met others who have experienced a similar path of unclarity and am drawn to guide them. Why do they trust a complete stranger? Maybe they are desperate and don't know which way to turn next just as I once was.

Today I'm still knocking on doors, learning new biochemistry and searching for radical thought leaders in this space. I'd rather listen to a great podcast or read a book on Mast Cell Activation than watch TV. I'm writing this chapter not because I'm an expert on any one topic but I am an expert listener, inquisitor, and researcher who is good at connecting the dots for people. This writing project was a personal mountain for me because writing doesn't come easily, but many of the best things in life don't either. I've procrastinated and put it on my calendar a hundred times. I've read paragraphs over and over and not absorbed what I just read. I promised myself no matter how long this took, I would not give up because I don't want anyone reading this to give up on their own health journey or that of a loved one. This matters to me—a lot. I want everyone to become their own most unrelenting advocate.

What would you do if you felt gripping fear after finding yourself asleep on the ground in the park? Would you take "everything looks normal" for an answer? I had to break the traditional patient/physician pattern, have faith in myself, be comfortable with not knowing, and embrace a path that was unclear. Now I'm fighting for all of those moms and kids who are walking my path. I want to educate them on how to break their own rules when it comes to their health.

My family still incorporates ideas that are radical to some, like intermittent fasting, keto meals, butter in our coffee, red light therapy, hyperbaric oxygen, inversion tables, and vibration plates. I have no doubt that my kids will be breaking their own rules one day or at least questioning them, and I'll be there to cheer them on.

Maybe one day I'll become a neuroscientist. Who says you can't go after that at 50?! It's never too late to go break some more rules.

BIOS

Cynthia Mollenkopf

Cynthia is a textile artist and owner of Cocoon Gallery in downtown Apex, North Carolina. A resident of the Triangle area since 1990, Cynthia feels fortunate to have found a home in local cultural arts boards, businesses, and events and strives to share the transformative power of art for makers, consumers, and communities. #shoplocalnc #triangleartworks #cocoongallerync

Rachel Murley, EA, Owner and Operating Officer for RKM Accounting and Tax LLC and The Accounting Joint LLC

Rachel lives in Missouri with her family with whom she enjoys spending time. She holds a bachelor's degree from Columbia College and obtained an Enrolled Agent status in 2017. She is a QuickBooks ProAdvisor and Certified Acceptance Agent with the IRS. With over 20 years in the tax and accounting industry, she started her own business in 2018 so she could help small business owners achieve their financial goals. Giving back and helping others is a core reason she finds time to volunteer with the Volunteer Income Tax Assistance (VITA) program and why takes part in philanthropic efforts when she can.

Kristy Cook

Attorney Kristy Cook, founder of the bicoastal Mod Law Firm, serves for-profit and nonprofit businesses in both North Carolina and Oregon with passion and dedication. As a mission-oriented person, nothing fulfills Kristy more than providing legal solutions for purpose-driven businesses, no matter their size.

Kristy developed her tireless work ethic at Drake Law School and Portland State University's Mark O. Hatfield School of Government and has spent the last decade of her career assisting for-profit and nonprofit businesses in achieving their goals. Kristy makes use of her diverse experience in the nonprofit, for-profit, and government sectors to help businesses overcome legal obstacles so they can focus on what's really important—their missions.

Chris Rinehart

Chris is the daughter of Judith Ann, the granddaughter of Carrie, and the great-granddaughter of Susan. A lover of national parks, bold colors, and old places, her personal mantra is: "You get more of what you focus on." This theory has brought blessings of robust love, laughter, and adventure into her life such as the time she encountered a grizzly bear while camping in Alaska. Ever curious, she graduated from Millersville University (in Pennsylvania) with a Bachelor of Arts degree in Psychology as well as Indiana University of Pennsylvania with a Master of Arts degree in Criminology. During the COVID-19 pandemic, she's learning to meditate and figuring out new ways to get a fitted sheet onto a mattress correctly the first time.

Crystal Candace Brown-Pinkney, Regional Vice President/Woman Business Enterprise/Owner

Crystal Brown-Pinkney is an accomplished owner and operator of a full-service financial services firm. She is an independent contractor and Regional Vice President (RVP) with Primerica Financial Services. With 20 plus years of experience in the financial services industry, Crystal is a fully licensed, register representative with PFS Investments Inc., currently licensed in five states. She also holds a life insurance license, representing Primerica Life Insurance Company in seven states to date, branching into additional states monthly. As an RVP, Crystal leads a growing team of independent licensed agents. Together their mission is to impact families with a solid financial plan, educating families by bringing Wall Street to *Main Street*. Their mission is to protect families with proper life insurance, to eradicate debt, and to help families become financially independent in at least one of two ways: by having money (investments and wealth building principles) working for them and/or by having a business (entrepreneurship) working for them or both.

Crystal is a graduate of Temple University with a bachelor's degree in business administration and a concentration in marketing. She attained level one ownership of her business in 2015. Her accomplishments include induction into the President's Council, earning the Financial Independence Council Watch award in 2005, and induction into the Financial Independence Council, earning the Power Builder Ring in 2020.

Marilyn Shannon

Marilyn is an experienced facilitator, author, superior court mediator, consultant, life/business coach, speaker, journalist, online TV/radio host, and the founder of Women's Power Networking. Marilyn is known as "the listener." She is a number one selling author for her book series, *In Just One Afternoon—Listening into the Hearts of....* Thus far, she has released books about men, twins, millennials, and people impacted by opioid addiction. Future book topics include divorcees, families who have lost children, black fathers, the greatest generation, and many more. In Marilyn's previous life, she taught special education in the public school system, owned a furniture store, and was a marketing and advertising representative for both print and television. Marilyn holds a degree in Communications and Public Address from Syracuse University and is a wife, mother of five, and Landon, Liev, Nolan, and Elon's grandma.

Marty Sloditski

Marty is a Certified Holistic Health Coach and HeartMath® Certified Coach. Through her health coaching practice, Master Your Stress, she helps busy professional women achieve a healthier, happier, more productive, vibrant life by helping them discover and implement solutions to conquer their stress. Marty retired in 2015 after a 16-year career in Human Resources. After leaving the corporate world, Marty, a lifelong Connecticut resident, moved to Apex, North Carolina, to be close to her three daughters and granddaughter and to begin the next chapter of her journey—starting her own health coaching practice.

Kristi Wiggins, ACC, "Neuroscientist wannabe"

Kristi is an ICF Certified Human Potential Coach and Food Scientist, specializing in neuroscience therapies, who teaches clients around the world how to empower themselves to change their brains. She is insanely curious, loves to connect with others and listen to their life stories. A loyal friend, wife, mother, and kid enthusiast. She spends a crazy amount of time cooking for her family and dreams of the day she can hire a personal chef. Considered by some, a serial entrepreneur, book junkie, foodie, and now an author (she never thought she'd say that). Will usually pick a book over watching the boob tube. She *loves* her family and all that it entails, and teaching what she has learned to anyone who will listen, as those before her have done.

Made in the USA
Las Vegas, NV
06 March 2023

68611314R00070